2017

D1209814

Better
by design

Better
by design
an introduction to planning and
designing a new library building

Ayub Khan

facet publishing

Published by
Facet Publishing
7 Ridgmount Street
London WC1E 7AE
www.facetpublishing.co.uk

Facet Publishing is wholly owned by
CILIP: the Chartered Institute of Library
and Information Professionals.

PEFC
PEFC/16-33-111
CATG-PEFC-052
www.pefc.org

Text printed on PEFC accredited material. The
policy of Facet Publishing is to use papers that
are natural, renewable and recyclable products,
made from wood grown in sustainable forests.
In the manufacturing process of our books,
and to further our policy, preference is given to
printers that have FSC and PEFC Chain of
Custody certification. The FSC and/or PEFC
logos will appear on those books where full
certification has been granted to the printer
concerned.

*British Library Cataloguing in Publication
Data*
A catalogue record for this book is
available from the British Library.

ISBN 978-1-85604-650-3

First published 2009

Typeset from author's disk in 11/15 pt
University Old Style and Zurich by Facet
Publishing.
Printed and made in Great Britain by
MPG Books Ltd, Bodmin, Cornwall.

Dedication

I dedicate this book to my daughter, Hawwa Jan Khan, who I hope might be inspired through libraries that she may encounter through her childhood and adult life, in a variety of settings: school, public, college, university or workplace.

Ayub Khan

Contents

Lists of figures and tables

Please note: Different regulations apply in different countries in relation to architecture and construction. Always consult the local regulatory body for every new building or refurbishment project.

Preface

First we shape our buildings and afterwards our buildings
shape us.   (Winston Churchill, 24 November 1951)

The design of a library profoundly affects the experience of its users, in exactly the way the quotation above suggests. The design will set the tone for the environment and the ethos of the facility and will contribute to the total library experience of all users and staff. Physical spaces are changing as a result of new technologies, and student-centred approaches to learning have led to a need to rethink library design.

However, libraries of the 21st century are no longer simply repositories for print-based materials and books. They have changed and expanded, been rethought and redesigned. Libraries now provide an increasing range of services and facilities, using a multitude of media to reach a more diverse audience than ever before.

The developing role of the library has created a set of new and complex challenges for those delivering library buildings and services. There is no such thing as the 'perfect' library building. However, a well designed building may enable a project both to gain local acceptance more easily and to ease the process of securing planning permission. It should also support the parent organization well and offer a better service to users than the building it may replace. It should be more efficient to run than any former building and be easily adaptable to a different use if no longer required. The process of creating a new library is therefore one of the most complex, challenging and fulfilling activities that an individual or organization can undertake.

Although the word 'library' is used, and this continues to have a strong brand, a number of institutions have chosen to use a different word for their buildings. Examples include: learning resource centre, learning hub, information centre, learning mall, knowledge place, multimedia centre, ideas store, book bar, cultural centre or some kind of 'forum'. The term 'library' in this book could denote all of the above.

This book aims to steer a path for library practitioners through the planning of new library buildings and facilities. It is meant for beginners, not only for people new to the library profession but also for skilled and experienced practitioners who are approaching for the first time the important task of creating a new library or major refurbishment or re-modelling of existing facilities. Its starting point is that few architects in such a situation know very much about libraries, and far fewer librarians know about architectural planning and design.

This is not a comprehensive buildings manual. It is intended to be a guide to the language and processes that librarians may need to understand, as members of a team overseeing a new library building project.

Learning from past experience and investing in time during the early stages will help to achieve a positive outcome. The following advice should be borne in mind at the start of any major project: 'Design quality need not cost more money, and often it is the appliance of higher aspirations, more thought and greater skills that deliver the better projects' (CABE and Resource, 2003, 3).

Ayub Khan
Head of Library and Information Services (Strategy)
Warwickshire County Council

Acknowledgements

The author would like to thank the following individuals for their contributions to this book:

- Stella Thebridge for assistance with research and editing
- Brian Edwards for permission to use material we have worked on together for a chapter on libraries and information centres in *Metric Handbook* (Edwards with Khan, 2008)
- CABE for permission to draw on material in *Creating Excellent Buildings* and other CABE publications
- DEMCO for supplying the images relating to spatial measurement used on pages 132-6
- RIBA for the use of material in Figure 5.2 and Table 6.2 (see acknowledged sources).

The following individuals kindly read through draft versions and submitted helpful comments:

- Tom Bolton, Research and Futures Advisor, CABE
- Guy Daines, Director of Policy and Advocacy, CILIP

- John Dolan OBE, former Head of Policy, MLA
- David Hammond, Design Director, Morgan Professional Services
- Will McMorran, Director, M&G Architects
- Judith Strong, enabler at CABE
- Sue Wilkinson MBE, prison librarian, Birmingham.

Every effort has been made to contact the holders of copyright material reproduced in this text, and thanks are due to them for permission to reproduce the material indicated. If there are any queries please contact the publisher.

Ayub Khan

Abbreviations and technical terms

There is a full glossary at the back of this book and every attempt has been made to explain abbreviations and acronyms in the text. Given below are the main acronyms used, for quick reference at any point from the text. Terms explained in the glossary are asterisked (*) in the text.

AIA	American Institute of Architects
ALA	American Library Association
Bookstart	Government-backed UK scheme administered by Booktrust to provide book packs for every child at ages 9 months, 18 months and 3 years. Most authorities have a Bookstart Co-ordinator who also co-ordinates activities for under 5s in libraries and children's centres
BREEAM	Building Research Establishment Environmental Assessment Method
CABE	Commission for Architecture and the Built Environment
CDM	*construction, design and management
CILIP	Chartered Institute of Library and Information Professionals

DBERR	Department for Business, Enterprise and Regulatory Reform (estd 2007, taking some responsibility from DfES, *q.v.*)
DBFO	*design, build, finance and operate
DCMS	Department of Culture, Media and Sport
DCSF	Department for Children, Schools and Families (estd 2007, taking some responsibility from DfES, *q.v.*)
DDA	Disability Discrimination Act
DfES	Department for Education and Science (responsibilities allocated to DBERR, DCSF and DIUS in 2007, *q.v.*)
DIUS	Department for Innovation, Universities and Skills (estd 2007, taking some responsibility from DfES, *q.v.*)
HVAC	*heating, ventilating and air conditioning
ICT	information and communication technology
IFLA	International Federation of Library Associations
JISC	Joint Information Systems Committee
MLA	Museums, Libraries and Archives Council (formerly 'Resource')
NAO	National Audit Office
ODPM	Office of the Deputy Prime Minister
OPAC	online public access catalogue
PDA	personal digital assistant
People's Network	Name given to a government scheme to provide personal computers in every library in the UK for public use. The term is still used by public librarians to refer to their computers for public use.
PRINCE2	Project in Controlled Environments (project management methodology)
RFID	radio frequency identification (for circulation systems)
RIBA	Royal Institute of British Architects
SCONUL	Society of College, National and University Libraries

The word 'librarian' is used throughout the book to denote the person the architect would see as the 'client', that is, the person representing the organization that is leading the library building project. It is important to note that librarians might take on other roles in a building project, but in this book the term is used to denote the client (see page 45)

Chapter 1

Introduction

There is at least one thing that is certain about libraries. It is the uncertainty of what they will become in the future.

(Moshe Safdie, architect)

The planning of a new library can take as long as five years - so on the day it opens, a library already represents yesterday's thinking to some extent. Therefore, consideration of future needs - 'future thinking' - is very important. In the last 20 years, the library as a building type has seen many changes as it has adapted to accommodate digital information systems. This chapter notes some of the current features of different types of library.

Libraries today are facing the dual challenge of accommodating rapidly changing populations, and keeping pace with information and communication technology (ICT). ICT is altering notions of library space as well as communication links. Chapter 2 explores some of the recent trends in library development and the factors that have an impact on them.

Success is ultimately measured against a project's objectives, so these must be understood and shared by all the senior people in the organization. It is best to set down the vision for the project at the start and to refer back to it throughout the project. Chapter 3 looks at the development of a business case for a library project and suggests some strategies for ensuring success.

The creation of a new library requires the co-operation of a whole team, each member with his or her individual contribution to make. The constituents of the team, their relationships with each other and the way the project could be managed are discussed in Chapters 4 and 5.

Chapter 6 looks at the appointment of an architect. Both the librarian and architect will need to contribute unique skills to ensure that a project is successful, so a positive relationship between the two is vital.

Increasingly, library services are offered in dual or multi-purpose settings, for example within a school or other community building. At the same time, new funding streams are opening up to libraries, especially in the public sector and particularly where there is evidence of partnership work or community engagement. Chapter 7 explores these issues and their impact on library design and building.

Chapter 8 describes the design brief, the single most important document in the design process, and Chapter 9 looks at design quality, exploring the elements of urban, building and interior design.

As library use changes, so does the allocation of space within the building. Chapter 10 looks in some detail at space planning and accessibility.

Finally, Chapter 11 considers occupancy – moving in – and post occupancy evaluation – learning from the experience and gaining evidence to support the development of further projects.

Reference is made throughout the book to different types of library and much of what is discussed applies to any library. All will have varying amounts of public space, available to all, and back-room space where staff work to service the needs of the visible part of the building. The main types of library and their key features are listed in Table 1.1.

Different types of library have different emphases and relationships between them. For example, university libraries need to balance the needs of the teaching, learning and research communities. The Director of the OCLC Network encourages library managers to question why libraries exist: 'The constant questioning of a library's reason for existing

Table 1.1 Types of library and their key features (adapted from Edwards with Khan, 2008)

Main types of library	Key features
National library	National collections of books, journals, maps etc. Research focused Conservation element Specialist readership
Public library	Collections – books and other media – primarily for loan, but also reference Computers for public use (People's Network) Family history material Local and community information Often integrated with other 'cultural' buildings Wide range of customer base
Academic library	Study support for teaching and learning Research collections Large computer areas Often 24-hour access
Professional and special libraries	Specialist collection of books and professional journals Often contain rare material Limited access facilities Conservation element Closed community of users

is a very good thing. Libraries have continued to evolve to find their appropriate function – their core service. They will continue to get funded and continue to exist' (OCLC, 2003).

Chapter 2

21st-century libraries

In the 21st century, library planners and architects have an opportunity to create new facilities designed for a new audience. It is important to consider the forces that are changing library design and how these changes can be accommodated. This chapter considers some of the recent trends in library design, and issues to consider when planning a library for the 21st century.

[A library is] at once a school, a home, a workplace, a church, a theatre and many other things besides.
(Francine Houben, 2002, quoted in Latimer and Niegaard, 2007, 69)

Recent library developments

Towards the end of the 20th century there was a significant increase in the number of new and refurbished library buildings, including public, national and academic libraries. Some notable examples include:

- public libraries in Peckham, London (architects: Alsop and Störmer), in Brighton (LCE architects) and Vancouver, Canada (architect: Moshe Safdie)

- the Bibliothèque Nationale national library in Paris (architect: Dominique Parrault)
- the Thames Valley University library, designed by the Richard Rogers Partnership and the Squire Law Library, University of Cambridge (architect: Foster and Partners).

The three main reasons for the revival of interest in library buildings at this time were:

- new media technologies leading to a re-assessment of the role of libraries in a digital age
- other cultural buildings, particularly museums and art galleries, being seen as worthy of interest in their own right as buildings, rather than merely for the collections they contain
- the expansion of higher education worldwide with academic libraries having to change their role to support new methods of teaching and learning.

The main factors leading to change in the design of library buildings are:

- libraries as a statement of a knowledge-driven society
- new information technology especially electronic data collections
- a greater community and educational role for libraries
- the expansion in higher education and growth in life-long learning
- the impact of popular culture on libraries
- the increasing importance of library buildings as visitor attractions.

Changes to the storage and dissemination of knowledge may alter the form and content of libraries but they have never made the library redundant, despite predictions to this effect. In fact, the evolution from the scroll to the hand-written book, printed book, mass-produced scientific journal and internet has tended to increase the importance of libraries, which have proved themselves able to adapt to each new technology. The internet has opened up access to library resources across the globe.

However, the shift from a purely print-based library collection to one of mixed media, particularly those delivered electronically, has profound implications for library design. Library planners now need to consider:

- the role of reading and relaxation areas in an ICT library
- the function of silence in a library dedicated to team-based learning
- the balance of provision between social space and study space
- the concept of separate rooms as opposed to a large open space for digital interaction.

Libraries remain centres for information, learning and culture, and planners need to consider the mix of provision their users require, for example, social spaces, separate rooms, snack bars and cafés, study collections, children and family areas. They need also to remember that the building fabric could be a learning resource in its own right alongside the materials that are housed there.

Changes in the delivery of information in modern libraries affect every aspect of the planning process. In a recent publication on library design (CABE and Resource, 2003) the changing nature of library architecture was neatly summarized as shown in Table 2.1. This demonstrates the need to review the thinking about library design for the 21st century and to keep designs as flexible as possible.

Table 2.1 Library architecture (adapted from CABE and Resource, 2003, 4)	
Traditional	Modern
Hierarchical design and circulation	Open-plan design and circulation
Imposing steps and entrance	Street-level, retail entrance
Domes and rotundas	Atriums and top-floor cafés
Restricted access to books	Open access to books and other material
Temple of knowledge	The 'living room' in the city
Institutional furniture	Domestic or club furniture
Stand-alone building	Shared space with other services
Librarians as knowledge custodians	Librarians as knowledge navigators
Child free	Child friendly
Galleries and mezzanines	Escalators and lifts
Individual study carrels	Seminar rooms and computer suites

The fundamental design of libraries has changed over the years. Often in the past libraries were designed so as to utilize maximum wall space and with minimum natural daylight. Thinking has changed, as shown in Figure 2.1 below. The diagram on the left shows the traditional library model: readers are enclosed by knowledge with the walls of the library housing books and other resources. There is very little natural light.

The diagram on the right shows the new model, with knowledge at the core of the layout and readers surrounding the resources, thereby able to enjoy the natural light and views to the outside.

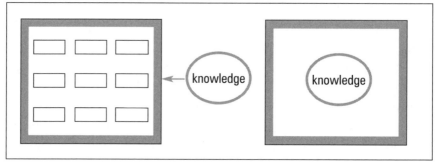

Figure 2.1   Changes in library layout

Planning for now and the future

Along with other types of social institution, libraries are changing rapidly. This makes it particularly difficult to plan appropriately for the needs of users over the next 50 years or so. Librarians may be aware of changes linked to automation but may have overlooked other recent developments, for example, the move to collaborative learning or the impact of demographic change. Some of these issues, and their significance for library planning, are explored below.

Partnership

In future, it is likely that libraries will be developed in partnership with other organizations or services, from commercial supermarkets to adult education providers. With government expectations of a rise in the number of students, so that 50% of those under 30 will go into some kind of further or higher education by 2010, there is increased pressure on educational institutions to adapt their facilities. More multi-purpose libraries have been built, for example, public libraries linked to health centres, dual university and public library services, and combined school and public library facilities.

A partnership between Worcestershire County Council and the University of Worcester is creating a city centre cultural and learning quarter, incorporating a joint university and public library, children and young people's library, county record office and archaeological services.

'One stop shops' in public libraries are increasing in order to offer a wider range of council services via a library setting. Very few libraries are now being built as stand-alone facilities for a single sector. More information about partnership approaches and dual-purpose libraries can be found in Chapter 7.

Collaborative study

Whether a new building is to be a public, academic or other type of library, recent educational and management theory stresses that students should work together in teams, and group work is an increasingly significant dimension of education. Naturally, teams and groups need spaces where their members can work together. To accommodate this, library planners need to provide facilities in which five to ten people can work together to discuss a project, while not forgetting the need to provide appropriate spaces for one-to-one training as well.

Informal spaces where people can meet and talk are also important, by taking into account the library as a social space. Whether a public, school, or academic library, each is a community centre; students can benefit from studying together, and community groups can combine their research and deliberations. Computers, too, encourage collaboration and so should be included in the planning of group spaces. A modern library should accommodate an increase in collaboration between individuals and should support learning as a social enterprise.

Merging of media

> Somehow library managers, planners and architects seem
> fixated on the classic book-dominated library and have great
> problems redefining libraries for the electronic age.
>
> (Latimer and Niegaard, 2007, 31)

Another development over recent years has been the gradual disappearance of the demarcation of different media. This means that there is generally no longer the need for any separation of areas for different media, for example, a space for listening to audiotapes or another for watching a video. Even media equipment tends to be multi-functional. This means that service points should also be multi-functional. It is no longer acceptable customer service to send library users from one desk to another. There is nowadays little reason to locate the microform desk and collection on one floor while the audiovisual department is housed on another. Combining service desks is also a cost-saving measure to be borne in mind by library managers. Planners are now encouraged to integrate different types of media in the same area and to move away completely from the idea of desks or sections for a particular medium or technology. Layouts nowadays are more likely to be designated by subject content (e.g. science), audience (children) or usage (quiet study).

Service integration

If a library is well established with separate departments, project staff will have to consider how to effect the transition to a new model of media integration as smoothly as possible. Not only do customers profit from the consolidation or clustering of services, but it may also be possible to keep more services available during evening and weekend hours when staffing levels are lower and costs may therefore also be lower. Such integration may create problems if staff are unfamiliar with particular types of equipment or technology. Professional librarians and information workers are increasingly working across a range of subject areas or disciplines. All staff need to be at ease with information retrieval through the vast range of resources available on the internet. Most will also have to train users in ICT skills. A new library project will necessitate an update of staff skills, particularly those involving ICT and the competencies associated with helping learners.

Changing demographics and library needs

Emerging multi-ethnic populations in many communities and the increasingly urgent need for literacy and ICT skills are new factors necessitating change in the design of library buildings. The library design should celebrate the diversity of its population. Early consultation with communities is essential, and community views should be reflected in the art, collections and choice of architect for the building.

For people who do not have English as their first language and for individuals who are newly arrived in an area, the library may be an important point of contact with their neighbourhood. This may be true of both public and academic libraries where increasing numbers of overseas students rely on a library that can meet their learning needs. The architectural design may be extremely important in conveying an image of the library's ethos. The design must reflect the library's role as a gateway to learning and a 'shop window' of information and community services.

By 2020 it is predicted that half of the population will be over 50 years old, so the library has an important role to play in supporting the needs of older people. This has ramifications for the design and layout of library buildings, for example in the level of lighting and signage.

Design for children

Children's services will grow in importance as the library is perceived as a safe place to be in the locality. The library is safe not just as a physical space, but because access to electronic information is also safeguarded for young people. Projects such as Bookstart have demonstrated how important the library experience can be for very young children. The needs of children, young people and their families are subject to change and this must be reflected in the design of libraries. Spaces for children can no longer be an 'add-on' but must be integral to the library experience. Family-friendly public libraries are a growing requirement. Young people of all ages, and their parents, should be actively involved in the design of the service offered to them. Safety is a key issue to be resolved in any library design for young people.

Patterns of use

Library users may spend a great deal of time in private study, whether they are formal students or 'non-academic' users of a public or specialist library. There is, therefore, growing demand to provide facilities of a non-library nature within the building. These might include a café but could also include gallery space for displaying local art works or community projects. As libraries broaden their social role to become 'ideas stores' or 'discovery centres' there is pressure to increase the extent of what has traditionally been regarded as non-library accommodation within their walls.

In some cases, libraries may offer facilities akin to a social club. Libraries could become key communication centres for transient populations, and their design will need to reflect different styles of use, for example, hot-desking, browsing, long-term study. In addition, the continued rise of the one-person household (from 18% of households in 1971 to a projected 36% in 2016) could encourage libraries to be key meeting places for their communities.

Supporting the development of literacy skills

Most libraries are now active in developing the reading and literacy skills of their communities. This has an impact on the way that materials are organized and displayed. So-called 'power' displays and face-on shelving are important in highlighting stock. Stack areas should have overhead line-of-sight subject signs in the aisles so that users can navigate through the library. The design for a new library should explore the means to achieve maximum capacity while displaying stock in an attractive manner. Libraries are increasingly looking at the way the retail sector both displays products and provides customer access. (For more information on signage, see Chapters 8 and 9 and Appendix 3.)

The virtual library

Planning for the future needs to take account of rapid changes and advances in technology. Traditionally in libraries, ICT has been used to increase efficiency in some key processes (circulation control, self-issue) and to increase the accessibility of resources (online catalogues, access to reference resources). In the future ICT will be fundamental to the experience of library users for learning and accessing information. Electronic links between home and libraries will increase, with a larger range of databases being offered by libraries via users' library cards. ICT can no longer be seen as an 'add-on' but must be an integral part of the service. It should be used everywhere in the library rather than being confined to one area. Wireless networks have made it possible for users to bring their own laptops and hand-held devices for use in the library. ICT can be part of the architectural make up of the building, e.g. video walls and access to virtual reality.

ICT development in libraries has been driven by a number of trends:

■ the change in society from an engineering/product society to a knowledge-based society and the associated thirst for information
■ the change in social interaction through different media
■ the change in attitude from the performance of certain tasks in certain locations to a more flexible allocation of space within a library
■ the increased use of mobile technology including laptops, mobile telephones and personal digital assistants (PDAs)
■ virtual library services provided 24 hours a day and 7 days a week.

Planning for leaner times

Amid the enthusiasm that accompanies the planning of a new library, it can be hard to remember that the pressure to maximize financial efficiency is critical. While budget cuts may lead to staffing reductions, cuts in book funds or the need to cancel journal subscriptions, a building project induces an artificial atmosphere of plenty amid harsh financial constraints. Suddenly the project team may find itself dealing daily with large sums of money, particularly for hardware and furniture.

The problem in many new library projects is that the construction budget – capital cost* – (for producing a larger building) is not always reflected in the library's operating budget – revenue cost.* When the new library opens its doors, the public will flock to enjoy its many attractions, but if there is no budget to support new or expanded services, this can lead to difficulties. In a recent example, a new central public library was planned with staffing based on a projected 5000 visitors a day. However, the day after opening, the number jumped to 9000. Moving the existing collection also required many additional staff hours, as did setting up and configuring the large amount of state-of-the-art equipment. Long queues became common at the checkout desk, and for a period of time it took more than a month for checked-in books to be returned to the shelves.

In any project, but especially when planning for leaner times, it is critical to plan for efficient staffing. Library staff numbers may be reducing or personnel shifting to undertake new roles. New electronic resources take an ever larger proportion of the budget or may enable an effective diversion of resources. It is important to design a library that can be staffed safely, efficiently and effectively by the smallest possible number of people. For example, stacks and work areas need to be arranged so that staff can use their time better, and control of light panels, security monitors and other equipment needs to be centralized so that the building can be operated effectively. Good design is integral to the achievement of effective staffing deployment.

Common elements of new library buildings

S. R. Ranganathan, known as the 'Father of Library Science in India', proposed five laws of library science (Ranganathan, 1931). These laws are:

1   Books are for use.
2   Every reader his or her book.
3   Every book its reader.
4   Save the time of the reader.
5   The library is a growing organism.

Since they were published in 1931, these have remained a centrepiece of professional values. Any new library development should consider them in relation to design criteria, particularly the idea of a library being a growing organism (that is, it requires flexibility and adaptability) and taking a user-centred approach to the design of the library, perhaps by following through a potential 'customer journey' in the new library. Noruzi (2004) provides a useful application of these laws to the world wide web, showing their continued relevance as basic tenets of library philosophy.

While considering the long-standing principles that are still relevant, the librarian needs also to consider the latest standards and recommendations for new libraries. Throughout much of the international literature discussing appropriate library design there are a number of elements that are becoming standard for new library buildings. The guidelines for developing public libraries set out by UNESCO and IFLA list a series of design criteria and facilities that need to be included in any moderately sized library.

They state that, in planning a new library, the following should be considered for inclusion:

- the library collection including books, periodicals, special collections, sound recordings, and video cassettes and other non-print and digital resources
- reader seating space for adults, children, and young adults to use for leisure reading, serious study group work, and one-to-one tutoring; quiet rooms should be provided
- outreach services: space should be provided to house special collections and preparation areas for outreach services
- staff facilities including workspace (including desks or PC workstations), rest space for eating and relaxing during breaks and meeting rooms where staff can meet with colleagues and supervisors in private
- meeting room space for large and small community groups which should have separate access to the washrooms and the exterior to enable meetings to be held while the library is closed
- technology including public access workstations, printers, CD-ROM stations, copiers, microfilm/fiche readers, public type-writers, and facilities for listening to recorded sound
- special equipment including atlas cases, newspaper racks, self-service book circulation, dictionaries, wall-mounted display

racks, display stands, filing cabinets, map cases etc.
- sufficient space for ease of circulation by both public and staff; this can be 15%–20% of public areas and 20%–25% of staff areas
- in larger libraries a café area for the public is a desirable facility
- space must be allowed for the mechanical services of the library, e.g., elevators, heating, ventilation, maintenance, storage of cleaning materials etc.

(IFLA, 2001, 44)

Brian Edwards and Biddy Fisher, in their book *Libraries and Learning Resource Centres*, draw together recent experience using a series of case studies, which show best practice in different types of libraries. From this research they offer the following insights (2002, xi):

- Libraries are essential buildings in cementing together communities of all types (city, village, academic, professional).
- Libraries remain meeting places but need to be designed to be more welcoming and accommodating to non-readers.
- I[C]T does not destroy the library but liberates it into providing new kinds of public services, attracting a potential new audience.
- The library is a knowledge channel which complements schools and college, and supports directly 'life-long learning'.
- For many the library is the vehicle of I[C]T skills transfer; the gateway for technological migration to society at large.
- As an institution the library is an essential element in a trilogy of investment in public services aimed at intellectual enrichment. Its partners include the art gallery and museum. All three are undergoing cultural transformation.

These perspectives point to a different type of library in the 21st century.

Summary

■ Libraries are responding to the needs of the 21st century by proving their ability to adapt to changing times; this provides exciting new opportunities in library planning and development.

■ It is essential to plan for the future as well as the present – changing demographics and the electronic revolution are two examples of issues to be considered.

■ It is also important to remember that capital expenditure in library buildings may take place alongside financially challenging times for the services themselves.

■ Many new library buildings are designed to be a focus for their communities, with space for meetings, outreach services, cafés and completely integrated ICT provision.

Chapter 3

Developing a business case

Before a project can start, it will usually be necessary to prepare a business case, to obtain management commitment and approval for investment in the project. The business case provides a framework for the planning and management of the business change; it also provides a tool for monitoring the viability of the project. This chapter looks at what the business case needs to include and suggests some strategies for ensuring success.

A library is not a luxury but one of the necessities of life.

(Henry Ward Beecher)

Content

The business case is the one document that encapsulates all aspects of the project's rationale – the what, how, why, when and where. Not all projects will have a business case but many have some type of rationale for the new library or re-modelling programme. It is crucial to check that the proposed project is clearly described, together with the benefits to the organization of the proposal. The business case should further clarify:

- that benefits of the project are consistent with the library's or parent organization's strategy
- that systems be established to measure success of outcomes, e.g. increase in visitor numbers, satisfaction rates
- that where there are options, the preferred option is clear, with reasons given, for example, the choice between a new library or a major refurbishment
- that where there is external procurement, the sourcing option is clear, with reasons given
- how necessary funding will be put in place
- how benefits will be realized
- any potential risks in the project and how these would be addressed. It may be necessary to undertake a high-level risk assessment in the business case, detailing the major risks of undertaking the project.

The business case should include five areas of information:

- strategic fit
- options appraisal
- commercial aspects
- affordability
- achievability.

The *strategic fit* should describe how the project will contribute to the organization's business strategy. Key objectives should highlight why the project is needed at this point, the key benefits and critical success factors, including the ways in which these will be measured.

An *options appraisal*, a means of considering several possible ways of achieving the goals of the organization, should be carried out to look at a minimum of three possibilities. The financial costs, benefits and risks of each option can then be compared and checked against issues of practicality and suitability. This would include an analysis of benefits that cannot be quantified in financial terms as well as identifying the preferred option and any trade-offs.

Options appraisal should also include assessment of alternative solutions, and there should be evaluation of their relative effectiveness, practicality, feasibility, cost and other factors. Options might include: a new build, extending the library, refurbishment or re-modelling and re-allocating existing space, converting a building for library use, or a mixture of these.

Commercial aspects would need to be included where there is external procurement, to outline the potential business arrangements. This section would need to include the proposed sourcing option together with the rationale for its selection. The key features of the proposed commercial arrangements would also need to be included, e.g. contract terms, contract length, payment mechanisms and performance incentives.

Affordability would include a statement of available funding and best estimates of the projected whole-life cost of the project, including running costs where applicable.

Achievability would comprise a high-level plan for achieving the desired outcome, with key milestones and major dependencies, e.g. interaction with other projects. This section would include outline contingency plans, e.g. for addressing any failure to deliver the service on time and major potential risks and an outline plan for addressing them. The provider's plans for these same contingencies would also need to be included, outlining the skills and experience required.

Information sources

The following sources would be used to inform the content of the business case:

- procurement documentation
- high-level programme and project management plans and documentation
- high-level requirements
- business strategy.

Ensuring success

In order to ensure the success of the business case, it is important to undertake thorough research and to look objectively at the plans, in order to understand the outlook from the management's perspective. If the finance director is to make the final decision about the project, it may be necessary to show how the benefits outweigh the costs involved. It may help to talk to a knowledgeable colleague in the parent body's finance department.

Although information will be gathered from a variety of sources, it is usually best to ask one or two members of the project team to write the business case. This will allow for consistency in the final document. It is important to remember the audience for the case and write to the appropriate level of expertise. Clarity and conciseness are paramount, and there should be little need for jargon. It is vital to communicate the vision clearly to the readership for this document. This may be helped by a key message such as: 'Being a part of the new community in X (a deprived area) is integral to the library service and council's policy on inclusion.' It is best to highlight outcomes rather than inputs.

The project objectives should be brief and limited to a few bullet points. The benefits to the organization should be stated together with any suggestions in the proposal that could lower costs or increase revenue. The benefits to key stakeholders must be identified as well as support of the longer-term strategic direction of the organization.

Any change to organizational processes should be noted, including effects on other departments within the organization. It is important to describe relationships with clients, external partners and competitors.

There should be a list of the resources needed to complete the project, including staff, hardware, software, print materials, time, budget and so on.

Finally, all the options should be given, together with the outcomes of each. These could include: effects on the service if nothing is done, stopping the activity, outsourcing and limiting the scope of the project. There should be a fallback position, for example, a phased roll-out of the programme.

In the case of a substantial change for the library, the librarian may wish to lobby individuals. It will be necessary to consider whether individual briefings of this nature are needed or some form of handout with brief points on it to promote the project.

In the case of a major building or refurbishment project, the parent organization may consider appointing consultants to help draw up a business case before committing significant amounts of money.

Figure 3.1 shows a sample form for stating the business case, showing the headings to be considered.

Please complete the form below and submit it to your senior project sponsor.
Background to the project (PLEASE KEEP BRIEF)
General aim(s)
Initial risks
Expected outcomes
Benefits of running with this project
Initial estimates of cost and time   £: Time:
Outcome of the business case
Decision from (*name*)
Date

Figure 3.1 Business case form

Risk analysis

An important part of the business case is assessment of the risks involved. There are considerable political, professional and financial risks involved in leading and managing a major project. Table 3.1 shows sample analysis which was undertaken for a new library project. Please note that this is not a full risk register, rather a couple of entries as an example.

Table 3.1 Examples of risk analysis factors				
Nature of risk or uncertainty	Likelihood high/medium/low	Impact high/medium/low	Likelihood x impact [score]	Actions required and who will take responsibility to manage the risk
Current site of library may need to be released prior to new library opening	2	2	4	Progress transition planning and investigate costing for temporary location (John Smith)
Design concept proves to be technically not viable	1	3	3	Validate concept design once design team appointed (Hawwa Jan Khan)

Score range is High = 4, Low = 1

It is useful to look at the business case for other projects to become more familiar with the format and style of these documents. One good example available on the internet is the document presented for the new Library of Birmingham. This is available at www.birmingham.gov.uk (search on 'Final Business Case').

Harriman (2008) is a new book taking library professionals through the whole process of creating and developing a business plan, and is worth consulting. This particular text has an accompanying CD-ROM of examples to help make the process even more straightforward.

It is important that there is a clear link between the vision and other aspects of the building process as depicted in Figure 3.2.

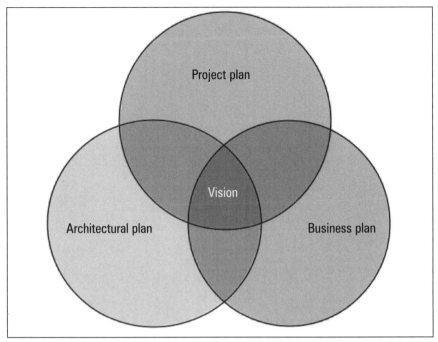

Figure 3.2   Inter-relationships of the building process

Summary

■ The business case is an important document, often required to obtain funding.

■ A good business case will clearly describe the project and include information about five key issues: strategic fit, options appraisal, commercial aspects, affordability and achievability.

■ Writing appropriately for the target audience, being clear and concise and demonstrating how the benefits of the project outweigh the costs are key to ensuring success, along with a focus on potential outcomes for all stakeholders.

■ Examining business case documents for other library projects will be extremely useful.

■ The business case should feed into the design brief.

Chapter 4

Project management

Project management is the application of good management practices in a structured manner. This technique can apply equally to both larger- and smaller-scale projects such as a scheme to introduce short-loan collections in an academic library, the implementation of a computerized issue system in a school library or resource centre or the creation of a new library. In this chapter the main components of project management are discussed.

In the case of a small-scale project, it may not be necessary to know all the detail in this chapter, but there are fundamental principles here for project management in general, not just in the sphere of library building.

Definition

When the term 'project' is used it conjures up a variety of images in readers but each has the following characteristics:

- a finite life-span
- a defined and measurable business product (what is being created – e.g. a new or refurbished library)

- a corresponding set of activities to achieve the business product
- a defined amount of resources.

A project also sits within an organizational structure with defined roles and responsibilities, where often the task is unique or non-repetitive.

One definition of project management is: 'a management environment that is created for the purpose of delivering one or more business projects to a specified Business Case' (PRINCE2, www.ogc.gov.uk/methods_ prince_2./asp). A more straightforward definition (offered by this author) might be: 'A definitive task undertaken to create a specific product or service'. This might be the creation of a new library resource centre.

There is no right or wrong way to manage a project. There is, however, agreed best practice to help increase the chances of project success. Many projects fail for a number of common reasons, including:

- lack of well defined requirements
- lack of communication
- lack of change control leading to 'scope creep' (the project taking on additional tasks and remit)
- lack of sound business reasons for the project
- lack of senior management commitment
- lack of planning.

Projects that are successful usually have defined deliverables (what will be achieved), well defined objectives and a worthwhile and viable business case. These characteristics are particularly important in building projects.

Projects need to have clear terms of reference, with agreed and measurable objectives. There will need to be adequate management and communication structures in place. It is also important to decide at the outset of the project how success (or failure) will be measured. A number of key performance indicators* (KPIs) need to be developed, for example, 'attract 2000 visitors a day'. It may be helpful to consider defined project values or guiding principles in conjunction with KPIs.

Stages in a project
Pre-project stage

The time before the official project start can be used to gather detailed information for the project board or sponsor (senior management) to make a decision on whether to commit time and resources to initiating the project. Developing a new library requires considerable expense and needs to be planned carefully from the start. A project board will need to be set up to manage the project strategically and make decisions. The size and scale of the board will depend on the organization and size of the project. The roles on the project team will be discussed in the next chapter.

Initiating the project

Once agreed, the official start of the project will establish fully the way in which the project will be executed and the detailed timescale. The document that is drawn up during this phase is known as a PID* (project initiation document). Once parameters have been set, the project board may decide whether or not to proceed further with the project. In the case of a new library project, this may mean taking a report to a board or committee to approve some early feasibility work and agree the scope and budget for the work with decision makers.

Directing a project

The project board will give advice and guidance, authorization and approval to the project manager to proceed with the project. Project boards may use management by exception,* to signal the specific problems requiring board or management attention. For example, it may be that a project is expected to exceed the finish date by four weeks. Any further delay would need to be sanctioned by the project board or senior management.

Controlling stage

This process falls within the remit of the project manager and is concerned with the day-to-day tasks of control and management. The project manager focuses on delivering the required quality product on time and within budget. A project plan should be developed and reviewed periodically; this can be done using special software or on paper. Projects need direction, management, control and communication to be successful. The project plan should include the work breakdown structures, project estimates and project schedules.

All projects should establish an effective communication structure; the size and scale of this will depend on the size and nature of the project. Managing communications, keeping information flowing among members of the project team and the project board, helps ensure a successful conclusion of the project.

Managing stage boundaries

This is an important part of project management which focuses on reviewing what work has just been completed and the resources that will need to be committed to the next phase of work. Some projects may use 'gateways' as a method of managing boundaries, particularly in the public sector.

Managing product delivery

This process also falls to the team manager. The work of creating the product is done here and may be carried out by external suppliers (e.g. the architects). This process provides an interface between the project manager and the supplier. It is really important that any product descriptions (what needs to be created or changed) are clear and unambiguous. Producing the brief for the architects will be crucial to the success of any project.

Closing the project

This final process is to ensure that the project is completed in a controlled manner. The project manager will tie up any loose ends and report on and evaluate the project. All project files need to be filed for auditing purposes. It would be helpful formally to record any learning points during the process of the project.

Decision making and financial controls

Two further aspects of project management need to be noted: decision making and financial controls. During the life of a capital project there will be several occasions when decisions have to be taken quickly (without the time to refer to a board or steering group). One example is when a building component is not available and an alternative needs to be ordered at short notice so as to keep the contract on time.

Costs fluctuate and change as decisions are made. It is important to keep control of expenditure and to be able to adapt the overall budget to take account of the variables which will occur.

Management of risk

Projects should identify the risks, assess the chances of each occurring, analyse the impact on the project or organization if the risks do occur, identify measures that can be taken to prevent them from occurring and identify contingency arrangements which can soften the effects. It is recommended that project managers compile a risk register, which is updated regularly throughout the life span of the project. (Note the section in Chapter 3 on risk analysis.) The following three points should be considered as part of the risk analysis for the project:

- assumptions
- dependencies
- contingencies.

Assumptions

Any assumptions that are made at this stage should be clearly expressed and recorded as these carry an element of risk (e.g. lending 10,000 CDs a year to generate a certain amount of income).

Dependencies

The risk analysis should include any dependencies or external factors over which the librarian has limited or no control (e.g. having three staff to manage and promote the collection, the library being open x number of hours).

Contingencies

If at all possible contingencies should be included in the project planning, for example planning an additional 10% to budget or length of project completion. Often they are cut, and additions are difficult to justify in today's financial climate (e.g. unexpected delay in opening, resulting in income shortfall).

Balance of cost, quality and time

All projects, large or small, have to balance cost, quality and time. The inter-relationships of the triangle (three measures) need to be carefully juggled through the life of any project. A decision on one will affect the other two; for example reducing the time may affect the cost and quality of the product; reducing the cost may affect the quality and extend the time taken to complete; reducing the quality may save money and time but will have an impact on the outcome and, in particular, on the durability of the finished product (see Figure 4.1).

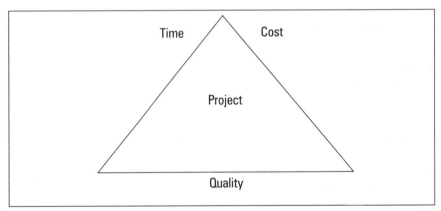

Figure 4.1   Time, cost, quality balance

Time management

It is vital to allocate sufficient time to each stage of the project. The finished building will need to last many years. Its effectiveness will reflect the amount of time expended on the planning processes. Time will be needed to assimilate background information about the construction industry and the role of the architect. The process of understanding the project's potential will take time, and consultation will always take more time than one imagines.

At the start of a project the end may seem so far away as to feel unreal. Sometimes a great deal of time will be invested in a feasibility study that concludes that a new building is *not* the answer. Even if a feasibility study does show that a new build is the way ahead, considerable time will still be needed at this early stage to examine design options, methods and potential risks. The librarian will need to ensure that enough time is allowed to:

■ explore options
■ collect data on which to base decisions
■ communicate carefully to all concerned
■ decide what help to seek
■ start to develop an outline brief.

As well as organizing her/his own part in the construction project, the librarian will also need to think at this point about how the building will be managed once it is open.

It is essential to plan realistic timescales. Projects often take longer than a client expects. Practical challenges may cause delays; negotiations with funders can take longer than expected. In reality, for a large building, five years from first thought to occupation is common and even small projects can take two years or more. For example, in a medium-size project, time could be taken as follows:

Initial planning, site acquisition, and financial approvals	12 months
Design – tender (including securing planning permission)	18 months
Tender process and site preparation	6 months
Construction	12 months
Fit-out and move	6 months
TOTAL	4 years, 6 months.

Ensuring that appropriate resources are allocated for design is crucial. When the process does not allow sufficient time and opportunity for design consultation and feedback, the quality of the final project can be seriously compromised, with unfortunate results. If initial design has already been carried out, for example, in a school or institution where the library is part of a bigger scheme, the librarian needs to make special efforts to communicate with the designers once the choice of an integrated delivery team has been made.

Allowing for time towards the end of a project to absorb the impact of any unexpected twists in the process is also a wise precaution. It is best to avoid a rapid move or a public launch immediately after the programmed end of construction, as this will cause problems if there are unexpected delays. After handover the building systems are likely to need fine tuning and time must also be allowed for that. At the same time as commissioning these systems for use, time is well spent in obtaining feedback in the early days.

Figure 4.2 illustrates the point at which maximum value impact in the decision-making process can be gained.

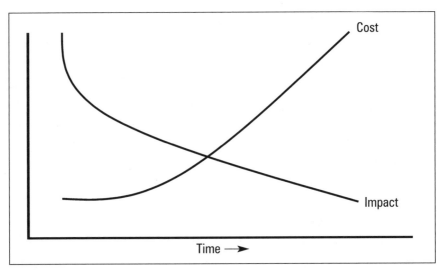

Figure 4.2   Time, cost and impact

Project management techniques

This is an outline of some of the techniques and terminology used in project management. The following website about PRINCE2 (Project in Controlled Environments) provides a structured methodology for effective project management and the UK 'best practice model'. The official site is www.ogc.gov.uk/methods_prince_2.asp.

CABE, in its best practice guide on how to commission a building project, *Creating Excellent Buildings* (Eley, 2003), provides a reliable resource for those about to embark on a construction project – whether beginners or experienced in the task. The most successful projects are those where there is both dialogue and co-operation between architect, interior design and library representatives.

Divided into the four main stages of a building project – preparation, design, construction and use – the guide provides detailed advice, including how to be an excellent client. Topics covered are:

- establishing the project vision, developing an outline brief and involving stakeholders in the process
- building the in-house client team, establishing roles and responsibilities, and managing the organizational change involved in a building project
- choosing a site or a building
- choosing the procurement route
- selecting the architects and consultant team
- developing the detailed design brief
- the client's role during the construction process
- preparing to use and launch the new building.

These should be incorporated in the project plan.

Managing change

It is important to consider change management as part of the library project. Library staff will have to adapt to a range of changes in terms both of the physical building and of routines and processes. For example, in recent years library staff have learnt to navigate new electronic data resources. Change management is a systematic approach to dealing with change, both from the perspective of the organization and on an individual level. Change management has at least three different aspects, including:

- adapting to change
- controlling change
- effecting change.

Change management is a key issue in the library project. The development of a capital project also has an impact by changing the environment in which service delivery takes place. It is important therefore to manage the process rather than be caught unaware by the impact a new building may have.

Change can be based on a strategy for the future or caused by external circumstances.

The development of a new library is an opportunity to consider how the organization wants to develop its delivery in the future and how that will then impact on the design solution. It is important that innovation in design is brought about through need and understanding of learning and how it will change and develop. Methods of teaching and learning as well as changes in curriculum need and demand have to be considered in the development of the project vision and in preparation of the brief to enable the design team to create an appropriate and innovative environment.

At an early stage consultation should take place to look to the future and consider how design processes can assist and influence positive outcomes and change.

It is important that end-user stakeholders are aware what is happening so they are not confronted with an environment that they cannot work in because they do not understand it. Consultation at the early briefing stages of the project is valuable in ensuring understanding and acceptance of the proposals by others. Design reviews and visits to other new facilities are also useful ways of increasing understanding of change. The design team needs to be involved in these activities.

Design has a huge impact on the way people do things. It is clear for example that if an entrance is moved and a route into or through a building is altered, it changes the way people use the building. So from the outset a new design is going to change the ways things are done.

Ensure time is spent understanding the implications before deciding on the solution. Try things out if possible, and visit places where these changes have already been effected. Visualizing design is now much easier with 3D visualization. This tool should be used to understand not only what a design will look like, but also how it may impact on use of the resulting building.

When planning to manage change there are some key principles that need to be considered:

- Different people react differently to change.
- Everyone has fundamental needs that have to be met.
- Change often involves a loss and people go through a personal process of negativity until there is a recognizable positive outcome.
- Expectations need to be managed realistically.
- Fears have to be dealt with.

It is crucial therefore to give people information in an open and honest way and to engage them in the whole process including decision making.

The organization will need to define and implement procedures and technologies to deal with changes in the working environment and to profit from changing opportunities that a new library or refurbishment may bring. One example might be the introduction of a self-issue system or RFID.* Staff will need to embrace changing working practices and processes in order to implement these new systems successfully. If the library project is to be successful, a programme of change management will need to be implemented.

The four key factors for success when implementing change within an organization are:

- *pressure for change* – demonstrating senior management commitment is essential
- *a clear, shared vision* – bring everyone on board; this is a shared agenda that benefits the whole organization
- *capacity for change* – provide resources of time and finance
- *action* – and performance – 'plan, do, check, act'.

Managers need to assess:

- their own role - leadership, communication, keeping informed, devolving responsibilities
- staff needs - respect for person introducing the change, opportunities to contribute, opportunities for training and personal development, means to effect change.

Throughout the process communication channels must be kept open.

Managing the process – key issues

Edwards and Fisher (2002) note that the planning team must be chaired effectively by someone with objectivity and understanding. They go on to describe key issues to address at each of three stages of the planning process, as shown in Table 4.1:

Table 4.1	Issues to address in the planning process (source: Edwards and Fisher, 2002, 39)
Early stage	Initial planning
	Involvement of others
	Consultation
	Defining and refining
	'Ownership'
	Staff involvement
	Experiences and innovation
Middle stage	Meeting and pressure of change
	Incorporating the views of users
	Technology
	Staff
	Organizations
	Transitional states
Detailed implementation stage	Agreeing performance targets (including architectural quality)
	Specifications for finishes and furniture
	Timetables for occupation
	Managing diverse expectations
	Understanding the contracting process
	Knowing what will cost money and time (especially late alteration to the brief or design)

The following pages give examples of forms and information for different aspects of project management: The project definition form (Figure 4.3 on the next page) is a summary of the project's parameters, the scope of the project, how it will be managed and high-level information about the project. Table 3.1 in the previous chapter gives some examples of the factors to be considered as part of a risk analysis of the project, and Table 5.1 in the next chapter is a checklist of activities that need to be project managed as part of a large-scale library building programme. This last is adapted from an early key text in library building design (Thompson, 1973; see Thompson, 1989). In *Creating Excellent Buildings*, Eley (2003) offers ten key success factors for the client in a projected new building or refurbishment – in this case the client is the librarian:

1 Provide strong client leadership.
2 Give enough time at the right time.
3 Learn from your own and others' successful projects.
4 Develop and communicate a clear brief.
5 Make a realistic financial commitment from the outset.
6 Adopt integrated processes.
7 Find the right people for the job.
8 Respond and contribute to the context.
9 Commit to sustainability.
10 Sign off all key stages.

Project management roles need to be considered. These include the management undertaken by the client – terms such as project sponsor and project co-ordinator are sometimes used. This document uses the term 'librarian' when discussing this role. The other type of management role is specific to the construction industry. In this case the project manager would be commissioned by the client body to manage the building project (a role sometimes undertaken by the architect but which is increasingly seen as a separate appointment, especially with larger projects). These are dealt with more fully in the next chapter.

Project title:	*Put here a very brief title*	Sponsor:	*Insert actual sponsor name*

State below the link with the corporate agenda – the actual wording please.

Put here the actual words in the corporate agenda – showing the link with this project

Project background:	*The background to the project. Give enough information to inform the reader.*
Project benefits:	*An outline of what the benefits are to the organization, individuals or stakeholders in delivering the project.*
Project objectives:	*The specific objectives for the project. Note: the objectives can be one line or more detailed text.*
Project deliverables:	*What will be delivered at the end of the project (e.g. a report, a building, improved service levels).*

This project will include:	This project will not include:
This section defines the boundaries of the project.	*Planning details should not be included at this stage.*

Figure 4.3   Project definition form

Success criteria:	*How the success of the project will be measured. Note: the success criteria must be measurable.*	
Constraints:	*Examples here can be specific (e.g. a skill which the project team must have, resources, or a legal deadline). Note: only include time and money if these can be quantified.*	
Key assumptions:	*The assumptions made in putting this document together.*	
Project manager:	*The name of this person and their tasks.*	
Project sponsor:	*The name of this person and their tasks.*	
Project board/ steering group members:	*Who fulfils these roles and what they do. Note: may not be appropriate for all projects*	Project team members:
Budget ❶		
Resource costs:	Other costs:	
e.g. construction equipment (furniture, ICT), new stock	Annual operating costs: *e.g. staff, ICT maintenance, energy consumption, cleaning*	
Total costs (attach a breakdown of the overall budget)		
VAT*– Some projects may have important VAT considerations. Have accountants within the parent organization been consulted?		
Start date:	Completion date:	
Signature of project manager:	Date:	
Approval from sponsor:	Date:	

❶ The librarian needs to liaise with finance officers in the parent organization in order to inform project delivery. The data on this form in relation to finance needs to be fine-tuned to organizational and project management needs.

Figure 4.3 *Continued*

Summary

- There is no 'right' way to approach project management, but understanding some of the elements of agreed best practice can be useful in any context, not just library design.
- It is generally agreed that projects go through various stages, from start to completion; understanding these will help project management.
- There are various tool kits and software packages specifically related to project management, PRINCE2 being one example.
- Strong leadership, clear aims, objectives and roles and being willing to learn from experience are important factors in project management.
- A good project manager will also have a good understanding of change management.
- Balancing time, money and quality are all important in ensuring an effective outcome.

Chapter 5

The design/project team

A successful project requires skilled people to work together in collaborative teams, inside and outside the organization, in order to design, cost and construct the project. This chapter explores the possible team roles, leadership and key tasks to be completed by the team.

Team roles

Many people are likely to be involved in a new library project and they must all have the right skills and ability to work in a team. Crucial to the project's success is the selection of the people and organizations, the definition of what is expected of each and the management of relationships between them so that they work effectively. As much work needs to be put into this as into discovering inspirational projects and best practice benchmarks.

The in-house team needs to involve people who understand the library manager's needs. Librarians who are new to the world of construction may also want to include within the in-house team an external person as a 'client adviser', whose experience will be helpful if they have worked in the past on a range of projects, not just libraries. This will give the library manager broad experience to draw on in helping set the project up, choosing design and construction professionals and assessing how far design proposals really meet project needs.

The wider project team needs to include a range of professionals, all of whom may be more or less involved at different stages. Success of the project and design quality depends on expertise found within various professions, including architects, surveyors, cost consultants, structural engineers, civil engineers, landscapers and construction teams. The skills of these professionals are interdependent and valuable for the members of a well managed team. Projects can be procured in a number of different ways and, although these may affect the team selection approach, fair, thorough, clear and transparent procedures are essential for any competitive selection. A carefully selected architect and/or client adviser should be well placed to support selection of other professionals. However, in all circumstances it is important to research the capabilities and past performance of potential consultants and contractors.

Teams may fluctuate in size and composition over time to meet the evolving needs of the project. It is important that all team members are clear about their roles and responsibilities; and lines of communication and rules governing team relationships must also be clear. Creating a clear decision-making structure and explaining it to all those involved will help to avoid misunderstandings.

Specialist knowledge will always be needed, although the number of people involved will depend on the size and complexity of the project. The following list includes the key roles in a large project (although many of them may be represented by the architect). This section is adapted from an early key text in library building design (Thompson, 1973; see Thompson, 1989) and advice from *Creating Excellent Buildings* (Eley, 2003), which describe roles in project teams.

Architect

The architect's team has overall responsibility for creating an environment in which the library and partnership organizations can optimally function, for the visual impact of the building and for its efficiency in terms of space use, structure and servicing. They should not simply devise a library building according to instructions received; they should visualize the future building both for its ability to deliver services flexibly in the long term and for its aesthetic contribution to the life of the community. Therefore a good architect will lead a consultant team that contributes solutions to the design needs, giving the client organization the opportunity to improve the building's impact, offer new amenities and obtain greater financial viability.

Design team

Architects rarely work as individuals, but will be part of a design team whose core members are:

- an architect
- engineers (structural and environmental or services engineers)
- cost consultants – normally needed at an early stage (see 'Cost consultant' below).

Others may be brought in as the project progresses. They tend to be appointed and remunerated on the same basis as the architect (see 'Specialist consultant', below).

The librarian

This person may act as the client in most cases, having the authority in all day-to-day decisions, being always in close contact with the scheme and keeping clearly before them the functional aims of the proposals. He or she will not necessarily be the chief librarian or service manager; however, in small libraries the librarian may have to fit the task of being the client into an already busy working life. In some projects there may be another member of library staff appointed to lead, who is authorized to make decisions about the project. If such a person is responsible for all library developments within their organization they will, in time, develop an expertise which can be of great value to their employer in future projects.

The librarian could take on other roles, for example be a project sponsor or administrator, but in this book they are seen as the client.

The project sponsor

The project sponsor is likely to be someone with significant authority who can, when required, represent the librarian. For example, in a local authority it could be a director of cultural services; in an academic setting it could be a vice principal. In small or simpler projects the project sponsor may also be the main promoter of the project, the design champion, even in some cases the practical leader, taking on the role of the librarian. In larger projects their role is more likely to involve supporting the librarian, communicating with the library organization, wider interest groups and with the media as required. Whatever the size of the project, the project sponsor needs to be forceful, a good communicator, politically astute, highly motivated and a shrewd decision maker. She/he will need to understand the needs of, and be accessible to, all stakeholders and have appropriate power, access to the librarian and time to carry out the role.

For a small but complicated project, a project sponsor may need to devote 50% of their time to the project, especially in the early stages. A larger project may need a full-time sponsor. Whatever the project and whatever the actual role, the project sponsor needs to be someone who can create positive team interaction and make people believe that the project should, and will, happen.

Note: The term 'project champion' became more common in capital projects when introduced by the National Lottery distributory bodies to identify the person who spearheaded a project. (This was often a board or council member who dedicated time and effort to pushing the scheme forward, but did not usually have responsibility for the day-to-day management.)

The project manager

The role of project manager can be included in the librarian's role but is significantly different. Therefore, for large or complex library projects the appointment of an experienced project manager is recommended. Such a person may be needed early on if the in-house management has limited experience. If appointed later, the project manager must quickly become familiar with the early stages of the project.

There are two types of project manager and either or both may be needed on a project. The main role of the first type is to look after the librarian's interests in relation to the technical aspects, to brief and manage other professionals and to be the 'employer's representative' with general powers to act on behalf of the librarian. This type of project manager has no authority under the building contract and cannot issue instructions to the contractor. They may be someone from inside the library with suitable experience, or be employed specifically for the role.

The role of the second type of project manager is to act as a contract administrator; they are named in the contract between the client and the contractor. This project manager has sole right to issue instructions and certificates, and the role therefore requires significant experience of construction projects; therefore the person is more likely to be chosen as part of the external team. In view of these enhanced powers, it is essential that a project manager in this role is fully aware of the librarian's 'vision'.

Cost consultant

Sometimes known as the quantity surveyor, this specialist is a key figure, usually employed at an early stage on the recommendation of the architect; the link between them will be close and ideally will have been developed through previous work together. However, in order to carry out their tasks effectively the cost consultant will work closely with all the various specialists concerned in the project.

The main task of the cost consultant is to estimate the probable value of the work and to assist the architect and the librarian in evaluating the various alternatives. From this information, the cost consultant will establish a cost plan, which ultimately, along with the design team's drawings, schedules and specifications, will form the basis of the construction contract. To do this they will need access to the architect's work at every stage and to understand the relative merits and costs of different constructional systems, details, materials and options in terms of contractual arrangements with builders.

From the beginning of the project, the cost consultant will be able to assist in providing budget estimates and evaluating options. As the project progresses, the work of the cost consultant develops into measuring and evaluating the entire content of the proposed construction works, and can often involve the preparation of a bill of quantities,* a type of giant shopping list for building contractors to price. At tender stage the cost consultant will provide a report on the tender prices received and advise on the choice of main contractor. During construction on site the cost consultant measures and quantifies the work in progress, providing valuations for the monthly interim payments to the building contractor. The cost consultant will also negotiate the final account. This is a reconciliation of the total building costs in relation to the original contract sum and all the necessary changes, additions and omissions carried out during course of the building work.

Specialist consultants

There can be any number of specialist consultants involved, depending on the size and complexity of the project and the problems that need to be solved. Examples of those who are likely to become involved are consultants with specialist skills and knowledge in structural and services design, heating and ventilation, acoustics, electricity, mechanical equipment, security, interior decoration and soil surveys. They may also include a fire engineer and experts in topics like the Disability Discrimination Act 1995,* ICT, community liaison and insurance.

Usually, specialist consultants will be recommended by the architect, who will ideally have previous experience of their work. On some projects the library or parent organization might have its own specialists, for example heating engineers. However the specialist consultants are sourced, it is normal for them to be employed on a contract direct to the library. This enables a level of independence so that, while the architect has access to the specialists, library staff may, if they wish, reject the advice. This ensures that any liability for advice given is not assumed by the architect but remains the legal responsibility of the specialists themselves.

Facilities manager

The role of the facilities manager is to set up contracts for, and be responsible for the day-to-day management of, services such as security, cleaning, deliveries and other activities that support the use of the building. Although this may seem a distant need at the beginning of a project, bringing a facilities management expert on board at the briefing and design stage can make a great difference to a library building in use. The operational aspects of the building over a number of years need to be considered in the design brief and will be an integral part of the contract to design and build the project. Therefore, while it may not be possible to hire the person who will actually manage the finished building, the expertise of a hands-on buildings manager can be useful at an early stage. This element is a key part of private finance initiative (PFI*) projects (also known as design, build, finance and operate* (DBFO) and part of the UK government's public–private partnership* (PPP) initiative), and could be particularly relevant in a large public or university library.

Administrator

Some projects will need a clerk or administrator, others will not, depending on the size and complexity of the project. Where such a person is in place, her/his role is to ensure the smooth administration of the project, keeping a record of decisions made and actions taken.

Planning officer or surveyor

In the case of a local authority, this officer will have an overview of the project and make recommendations to the authority based on planning policies contained in the local development framework. Key tasks may be completed during the early stages of a project, unless, as it develops, the planned use of space changes. Planning officers are likely to be heavily involved up to detail design stage and submission or consent of the planning application. The process can vary widely in complexity and may involve negotiation between the librarian, architect and planning officer.

Finance officer

The role of the finance officer is to oversee all estimates, payments and financial arrangements associated with the project. This officer will need to be involved throughout the project and will be responsible for all payments relating to the project. In order to do this effectively the finance officer will need to be kept fully informed at every stage.

Legal officer

Legal officers of the parent organization will be involved throughout the project, for example drawing up contracts; presenting reports to the authority, and making approaches to outside powers (e.g. ministries) where required.

CDM co-ordinator

Under the Construction (Design and Management) Regulations 2007 (CDM 2007) there is a legal duty for anyone carrying out building work to ensure that the project is safe to build, use and maintain, and that it delivers good value. It is therefore a statutory requirement to appoint a CDM co-ordinator to advise and assist in carrying out all CDM duties. CDM co-ordinators can be resourced from within the authority or by recommendation through the project manager, architect or cost consultant.

Current and future users of the library

The way that current and future users are represented will vary depending on the nature of the project. In universities and colleges, where staff and users are organized and identifiable, they may have clear representation through staff delegates and service users committees or reader groups. A similar arrangement may be possible in hospitals. However, in public libraries it is unlikely that general service users would be involved in the project team because:

- council members, who oversee all local authority activities, have been elected to represent the general public, the current and potential users, and within their role should have an opportunity to comment or participate
- the involvement of service users themselves at this stage can lead to self-appointed pressure groups exerting undue influence.

Although current and potential users may not be directly involved with the project team it is vital that wide consultation takes place if the project is to be successful; this is explored further in Chapter 7.

Strong leadership

> It is important to remember that enthusiasm and commitment are infectious and will contribute to a successful outcome. A successful project is usually fun most of the time for the people involved.   (CABE, 2003, 21)

All successful projects require strong leadership, in dealing with both daily tasks and those at a higher level. The librarian is the central figure and needs to ensure that there is a shared vision, with effective communication supported by clear structures, particularly with the architect. To do this they must be strong, have a clear view of what is to be achieved and be able to give and receive the necessary information at the right moments. They must identify clear priorities, set down when they must be consulted or informed and establish what is expected from everyone else involved in the project.

On many projects, effective leadership is provided at a higher level through a project board or steering group whose members, without day-to-day involvement in the project itself, have several roles. The effectiveness of this group will be significant in supporting the librarian's ability to lead the project 'on the ground'. The group will need to include the project sponsor and possibly other key members of the project team; however most of the project board or steering group is likely to be made up of people with high-level involvement, for example directors, elected members and senior representatives of stakeholder groups. An important part of their role will be to symbolize high-level commitment and encourage ownership of the project within their respective groups or agencies. To do this effectively they will need to:

- understand, and be committed to, the financial and other consequences of the project
- oversee the project in an advisory capacity
- monitor progress and communicate developments
- champion the project within their own groups or agencies and externally as required.

Through the work of the steering group and the librarian, the building and organization itself should remain central to the project with ambiguities, disagreements and hidden agendas clarified and resolved at all stages. This will ensure that everyone's needs are met and should avoid potentially costly complications.

Team activities

Table 5.1 lists the activities that may need to be considered or undertaken by the project team.

Table 5.1	Activities that the project team must consider (adapted from Thompson, 1989)
Setting up the project team	
Outline brief	Statement of aims
	Contents to be accommodated
	Activities and users
	Life of building, flexibility and expansion requirements
	Site location and limitations
	Security
	Communications
	Cost limits and controls
	Consents
	Time schedule (from client's viewpoint)
Feasibility study	Use of site – site investigation
	Space relationships
	Structural implications of space relationships
	Options appraisals
	Cost feasibility
	Feasibility report
	Outline planning
Detailed brief	Pattern of operations
	Verification and amplification of information
	Contract policy; client nominees
	Maintenance policy
	Planning principles redefined
	Division into major areas: reader circulation

Table 5.1 Continued	
Scheme design	Planning the structure
	Flexibility
	Structural grid: columns, sizes, spacing
	Floor loadings
	Service equipment: stairways
	Internal environment
	Construction
	Services
	Planning consent
Detail design	Layouts and critical sizes
	Book and resource accommodation
	User service areas
	Staff areas
	ICT
	Non-assignable areas
	Furniture and fittings
	Floors
	Circulation
	Lighting
	Enclosing elements and finishes
Security and protection	
Physical conditions	
Cost studies	
Final report	
Production information	Drawings, schedules and specifications
	Bills of quantity
	Tender action
	Project planning
	Operation on site
	Completion

The process of designing building projects and administering building contracts may be divided into a series of phases, shown in Figure 5.1. (Some variations of these phases apply to different types of procurement, e.g. design and build.)

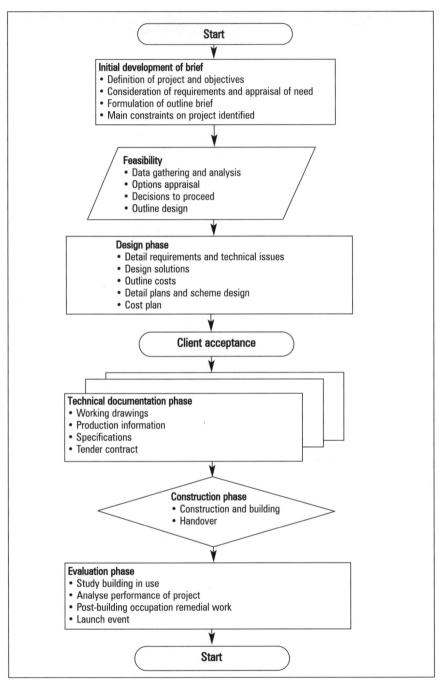

Figure 5.1   Main phases of a building project

A **Appraisal** Identification of client's requirements and of possible constraints on development. Preparation of studies to enable the client to decide whether to proceed and to select the probable procurement method.

B **Strategic briefing** Preparation of strategic brief by or on behalf of the client confirming key requirements and constraints. Identification of procedures, organizational structure and range of consultants and others to be engaged for the project.

C **Outline proposals** Commencement of development of strategic brief into full project brief. Preparation of outline proposals and estimate of cost. Review of procurement route. At this stage the general size, layout, appearance and cost of the building is emerging but not fixed.

Pre-construction
D **Detailed proposals** Complete development of the project brief. Preparation of detailed proposals. Application for full development control approval. At this stage the building form, particularly in exterior appearance and general interior spatial layout, is substantially fixed.

E **Final proposals** Preparation of final proposals for the project sufficient for co-ordination of all components and elements of the project.

F **Production information**
FI Preparation of production information in sufficient detail to enable a tender or tenders to be obtained. Application for statutory approvals.
F2 Preparation of further production information required under the building contract.

G **Tender documentation** Preparation and collation of tender documentation in sufficient detail to enable a tender or tenders to be obtained for the construction of the project.

H **Tender action** Identification and evaluation of potential contractors and/or specialists for the construction of the project. Obtaining and appraising tenders and submission of recommendations to the client. There remains a last opportunity at this stage to make modest changes to the content of the building and adjust the contract sum.

Construction
J **Mobilization** Letting the building contract, appointing the contractor. Issuing of production information to the contractor. Arranging site handover to the contractor. At this stage the contract is fixed, i.e. no change should be made if the overall project cost is to remain as agreed.

K **Construction to practical completion** Administration of the building contract up to and including practical completion. Provision to the contractor of further information as and when reasonably required.

L **After practical completion** Administration of the building contract after practical completion. Final inspections and settling the final account.

Figure 5.2 Work stages A to L (Phillips, 2000)

Figure 5.2 (page 55) identifies stages of work in the design and building of new and re-furbished buildings identified by RIBA's Architect's Plan of Work (Phillips, 2000). Architects usually work to defined strategies A to L, which represent a logical sequence of activities to be carried out by clients' consultants, specialists and contractors. Each stage allows each of these groups to discuss together particular issues of the building design (see Figure 5.2).

Summary

■   Many people are likely to be involved in the project team, sourced internally and externally. Each will bring a particular expertise.

■   A strong leader is crucial, with excellent communication and decision-making skills.

■   Consideration of the activities to be undertaken and the processes involved will help ensure the right people are brought into the team.

Chapter 6
Selecting an architect

Choosing the right architect is vital to a successful project. This chapter explores some of the issues to consider and ways to select and contract with architects.

The information that architects receive from librarians will guide them in detail, but there is a danger that, in providing the information, the librarian will assume that the architect is familiar with the type of library to be designed and built. In fact, an architect may assume that one type of library design will fit all, whereas librarians will know that different types of library vary enormously in their spatial requirements.

Firms of architects range from single practitioners to practices with a hundred or more staff. Some specialize in particular types of project. Some include in-house engineering or other design disciplines, for example, landscape architects or interior designers. Each firm will bring its own mix of skills and expertise to the project. A good architect will listen carefully to the librarian's ideas and attempt to turn them into a viable construction project.

The following is drawn from advice issued by the American Institute of Architects (Haviland, 2001) and from the Royal Institute of British

Architects (RIBA, 1999). Both of these professional organizations address some of the most frequent issues surrounding architect selection in clear documents. The information is also regularly updated on their respective websites.

General guidelines
Bring the architect into the picture as early as possible

Architects can help define the project in terms that provide meaningful guidance for design. They may also carry out site studies, help apply for planning permission, help locate funding sources, and provide a variety of other design services.

However, it is also useful if the client has already established the nature, size and scope of the project in outline and drawn up an initial briefing document. This will help to determine the type of architect practice they are looking for and to set the criteria for selection. If some form of competitive interview is used, the initial brief will help the architects focus their presentation.

Consider more than one firm of architects

The only exception to this would be if the librarian already has a good relationship with an architect and it makes little sense to change. Procurement regulation may preclude 'choice by experience'. However, many local authorities have an approved list of architects or in-house architects.

It is worth contacting other librarians who have developed similar facilities and ask who they interviewed and ultimately selected. Similarly, it can be helpful to find out who designed buildings and projects that are admired and/or seem similar to the proposal in hand. RIBA and CABE may also be able to offer advice. There are also a number of websites of international library architects that can be consulted. If the library project has a large cost threshold it may also be necessary to put an advertisement in the *Official Journal of the European Community*.

Clarify the information needed from architects

At a minimum, one should ask to see projects the firm has designed that are similar in type and size to the proposed project or that have addressed similar issues (for example, functional complexity, design aspiration or community involvement). It is not unreasonable to ask them to indicate how they would approach this project and who might be working on it (including consultants). They should also be willing to give out the names of other clients who might be contacted directly.

Consider a formal interview

An interview addresses one issue that cannot be covered on paper: the rapport between the librarian and the firm of architects. Interviews also allow the librarian to learn how each firm plans to approach the project. An interview may be with technical specialists such as structural engineers, planners and finance officers. The interview panel could include colleagues from other backgrounds, for example, urban planners, CABE, library specialists and other architects. The RIBA has drawn up a selection system which it calls 'the Competitive Interview' – details are available from the RIBA Competitions Office (www.architecture.com).

It is generally advisable to interview three to five firms in order to establish the range of possibilities without making the decision too complicated. Firms should be selected for interview on the basis of their expertise, experience and ability to bring a fresh look to this project. Each firm should be treated fairly, being offered equal time and access to the site and existing facilities.

The interview should establish how the architect's team will approach the project. It is important to ask how the architect will gather information, establish priorities and make decisions as well as to find out what the architect sees as the important issues for consideration in the project. The firm's style, personality, priorities and approach are all important and should be compatible with those of the library.

Alternatively, some firms could be screened out before the interview stage by completion of an application form or written tender. This should detail specific criteria required, for example, experience of work on a similar project, size of practice and turnover, number of staff (including specialists), approach to design quality and fees.

Make the final decision

Each firm needs to be told how the selection process works and when a decision will be made. If it has not already been done, past clients should now be consulted formally and in confidence about the firm's work and the performance of the resulting architecture. It might be useful to visit existing buildings to see them in use. This would also apply to the architect's office, in order to look at other projects and get a feel of how they operate. The selected firm, or short-listed firms, should be notified as soon as possible, as conditions like regulatory parameters, market conditions and team availability can change rapidly.

Personal confidence in the architect is most important. The ideal architect will provide an appropriate balance between design ability, technical competence, professional service, cost and a demonstrable empathy with the objectives of the development. Once the best firm has been selected, the legal department of the parent organization or local authority should help to draft the appointment, in terms of services to be provided and fees or remuneration paid for the full consultant design team.

Selection by competitive bid

It should be possible to ask for a fee proposal from an architect at any time during the selection process. Factors such as experience, technical competence and available staff resources will be important to the decision. If proposals are to be solicited from more than one firm, the librarian must provide consistent information so that the proposals received can offer the same scope of services, and can then be evaluated consistently.

Sometimes the sealed envelope system is used to separate considerations of design, quality of service, understanding of project and so on from the lowest bid. Architects are asked to prepare a fee proposal and bring it with them to the interview – all envelopes are opened after the applicants have been assessed on the quality criteria. Fees can then be negotiated taking account of all the bids made.

Fees are likely to be expressed as a percentage of the project cost.

Fixed tenders are normally offered by design and build or in response to a well developed brief. Even then, they are likely to have a significant contingency built in so may prove more expensive in the long run.

It is important to find out how prospective architects do business, how they work with their clients, how responsive they are to library management and decision styles, and how well they perform against their clients' expectations. The architect is a professional who will bring experience and specialized knowledge to the proposed project. The librarian should feel able to ask the architect these questions:

- What does the architect expect to contribute to the project?
- How much information does the architect need?
- How does the architect set priorities and make decisions?
- Who in the firm will work directly with the librarian?
- How will engineering or other design services be provided?
- How does the firm provide quality control during design?
- What is the firm's construction-cost experience?

Openness and honesty are crucial. It is vital that the architect understands the librarian's own knowledge and expectations. He or she should always be able and willing to explain anything the librarian does not understand. The more that is known at the outset, the better the chances of a successful project. A good architect is a good listener. Only when concerns have been outlined can the architect address them.

It is essential to confirm the ability of the architect and individual co-consultants to stand financially behind the services to be provided. All registered architects are required to carry professional liability insurance much like that carried by doctors, lawyers and accountants.

Most clients make professional indemnity insurance a mandatory requirement – but some set it too high for the scale of work and thereby preclude some of the firms that might be best suited for the type of work. It is a good idea to take advice on what is appropriate for the job in hand.

The librarian needs to be able and prepared to answer questions about the project's purpose, budget, timeframe and site, and the team who will be involved with the project. Again, it is important to be open and to inform the architect of any information that is to be kept confidential.

Selection as a mutual process

The architect will also be selecting the librarian as their client in this project. They are as interested in working on a successful project as the librarian, and they know that good architecture results from empathy between architect and client.

Even the simplest of projects can become complex because of the people involved, service needs, site, financing and regulatory requirements. Many of the librarian's needs and expectations may come into focus only while formulating the design. It is vital that the architect and librarian communicate regularly and effectively throughout this process.

Payment and fee systems

Experienced clients recognize that adequate remuneration for the architect is in the project's best interest as it assures the type and level of services needed to fulfil service expectations.

The amount of payment to an architect depends on the type and level of professional service provided. More extensive services or a more complex or experimental project will require more technical research by the architect and increase project costs. It is important to budget accordingly.

The method of payment will need to be negotiated, but the following methods are commonly used (compensation may be based on one or more of them):

- *percentage of cost of the work,* in which payment is calculated by applying an agreed percentage to the estimated or actual cost of the work, whichever cost is most certain at the time the calculation is made
- *multiple of direct personnel expense,* in which salaries plus benefits are multiplied by a factor representing overhead and profit
- *professional fee plus expenses,* in which salaries, benefits and overheads are the expense and the fee (representing profit) may be a multiplier, percentage or lump sum

- *hourly rate,* in which salaries, benefits, overheads, and profit are included in rates for designated personnel, e.g. director, senior architect (This makes good sense when there are many unknowns. Many projects begin with hourly rates and continue until the scope of the project is better defined and establishing another basis of compensation is possible. It may also make sense to use this approach for contract administration and special services, such as energy and economic analyses.)
- *stipulated sum* for the project – a lump sum (This is a matter of negotiation with the architect, but generally it includes the architect's direct personnel expenses (salary and benefits), other direct expenses chargeable to the project (such as consultant services), indirect expense or overhead (costs of doing business not directly chargeable to specific projects) and profit. The stipulated sum does not usually include reimbursable expenses.)
- *square footage* – the square footage of the structure multiplied by a pricing factor; often used to estimate 'ball park' costs during the initial stage of a project
- *reimbursable expenses* – out-of-pocket expenses incurred by the architect on behalf of the owner, such as long-distance travel and communications, reproduction of contract documents, and authorized overtime payment. Detailed in the owner–architect agreement, they are usually in addition to payment for professional services and are normally paid as they occur.

Once the method and amount of payment have been established, the architect should be asked to provide a proposed schedule of interim payments. Such a schedule will help the librarian plan for the financial requirements of the project.

There will be other costs beyond the librarian–architect agreement. These include site surveys and legal descriptions; geotechnical services; archaeological studies; technical tests during construction (for example, concrete strength tests); an on-site client project representative (clerk of works); and the necessary legal, auditing and insurance advice services needed to fulfil the owner's responsibilities. It may also be advisable for the architect to attend public meetings and undertake presentations on the scheme to key stakeholders throughout the project, and this will need to be built into the costings. If a fly-through (a computer animation of a building) or model of the building is required, this cost will also need to be built into the budget.

Design competition

On large-scale projects, librarians may wish to set up a design competition between a small group of consultants. The consultants are asked to submit their designs with estimates of fees and/or constructions costs. If the designs are paid for at cost this can be a good way to obtain a selection of designs, including the quality and scope of the work proposed, with cost implications. However, it can be expensive and can also mean that too much emphasis is put on design and technical factors; these also need to be balanced with managerial ability.

Design competitions can produce variable results and sometimes place unreasonable demands on the architects who take part. There are a number of procedures that have been developed over the years and endorsed by representatives of client bodies, professional organizations and government which (when required) comply with EU procurement legislation. A winning scheme in a design competition might fail to get planning approval. To reduce the chances of this happening, the brief-writing stage should include discussion with local planners. The risk of a competition design being denied approval is no greater than with other designs.

The procedures for competitions range from the competitive interview (mentioned earlier), to the full-scale design competition. The latter is relatively rare - a more usual procedure, where initial design work is required, is as follows:

- Draw up a long-list (advertisement, research, recommendation).
- Ask for 'expressions of interest' (details of previous work, design philosophy, practice skills etc.).
- Short-list against given criteria.
- Arrange site visits and interviews.

■ Select a limited number (say, three) to prepare outline designs in response to an initial brief.
■ Ask technical assessors to study submissions and prepare a report.
■ Invite finalists to present the designs to a panel.
■ Select architect and team.

Where architects are asked to prepare designs (as distinct from outlining how they might approach the job at interview), it is recommended that they receive some payment – an honorarium of some sort is more usual than stage fees (i.e. working up design details to a certain stage (see Figure 5.2 on page 55).

The competitive interview works well for a wide range of types and scale of projects. The interview or design competition has been used very successfully for larger and publicly significant projects.

The RIBA offers both advice and, if required, a full management service (for which it charges a fee).

Criteria for architectural selection

To enable effective selection, the librarian will need to decide at the outset how architects' proposals will be assessed and the weight allocated to different criteria, for example cost versus quality. Some organizations have procurement departments and/or policies which will help with this process.

It is also important to consider at an early stage how the library team will work with the architect, as this will have an impact on the cost and quality of the project. For example, the architect may design the building from an initial brief; alternatively she/he may work alongside the team throughout the project.

Whatever selection processes are used, it is important that the architect is:

■ technically competent
■ financially stable
■ operating sound health and safety policies
■ of sound reputation

- good to do business with
- able to share the librarian's project vision.

Figure 6.1 lists examples of criteria used in the selection of architects for a major new library.

Experience of and interest in designing public buildings and their surroundings which have a strong civic role and ability to attract wide and diverse audiences
A demonstration that the architect has understood the problems of designing an important public building which is central to a major regeneration area and the broader promotion of the city as a leading national/international business and cultural centre
Sensitivity to the relevance of creating an architectural icon to achieve these objectives
A demonstrable success with, and interest in 'knowledge economy' buildings where learning and non-formal educational requirements are paramount
An ability to rapidly engage with complex patterns of public interest and use, particularly the ability to articulate how the building design relates to a wider public area, which is seen as a learning quarter
Experience relevant to the detailed key design issues identified
Expertise in sustainable design not only in terms of practical issues but also its philosophical importance in terms of sustainable and liveable cities
Interest in and commitment to the process of gaining public, political and other support for the project
Ability to work with and communicate effectively with client and other consultants over a long period, giving this project the priority it will require
Resources to deliver the services in a reliable way

Figure 6.1   Example of non-technical issues in the selection of an architect for a major city library [Adapted from Birmingham City Libraries Prospectus, 2001].

Identifying the services needed

The experiences of others will provide helpful insights, but every project has unique features and requirements. The architect should be prepared to tailor the professional services available to meet the librarian's needs and expectations. Most building projects require design and construction documents, assistance in securing a contractor and evaluation of the progress and quality of construction. The services an architect can provide – in-house or through consultants – may include facilities programming; marketing and economic feasibility studies; budgeting and financing packages; site-use and utilities studies; environmental analysis; planning applications; preparation of materials for public referenda; special cost or energy analysis; special drawings, models, and presentations; and facility operation services after project completion.

Not all services have to be provided by the architect. Some parent organizations have expertise in project planning, design and construction and may, therefore, be capable of undertaking some project tasks themselves. Librarians may find it desirable or necessary to add other consultants to the project team to undertake specific tasks. Discussion with the architect will be necessary to establish who will co-ordinate librarian-supplied work or other services provided beyond the scope of the architect's agreement. However, this would need to be specified at the outset – the architect–design team relationship tends to be a specific and structured one.

The best strategy is to talk to the architect and identify the services needed. It is important to recognize that even when certain services are designated at the outset, other services may be required once the project is under way. Services may be added to an existing agreement at any time. A contingency budget should be set up to fund changes in the services required from the architect. Table 6.1 on the next page lists the types of services that architects provide. Note that different regulations apply in different countries.

Project specification

It is important for the specification to be right. Consideration to the following factors should be given when drafting a specification:

■ Avoid making the specification over-restrictive, as this may discourage some architectural firms from applying. It also discourages them from offering innovative alternative technical solutions. Sometimes it

Table 6.1 Services available from architects (source: Haviland, 2001, 8)		
Project administration and management services	**Evaluation and planning services**	**Design services**
Project administration	Programming	Architectural design documentation
Disciplines co-ordination, document checking	Functional relationships, flow diagrams	Structural design and documentation
Agency consulting and review approval	Existing facilities surveys	Mechanical design and documentation
Value analysis balanced with budget and programme	Marketing studies	Electrical design and documentation
Scheme development; monitoring of the work	Economic facility studies	Civil design and documentation
Evaluation of budgets and preliminary estimates of cost of the work	Project financing	Interior design and documentation
Presentations	Site analysis, selection and development planning; environmental reports	Special design and documentation
Construction management	Detail site space planning and zoning	Material research and sourcing, and specification

is better to specify needs rather than solutions (except where these are standard or recommended and tested practice).

- Ensure the specification does not contain features that directly or indirectly discriminate in favour of, or against, any supplier product or source.
- Avoid over-specification of performance expectations, e.g. more than are actually required to fulfil the purpose. This should also ensure that the lowest price is obtained.
- Ensure that all necessary information is included, but exclude any that is unnecessary as this may cause confusion to the person submitting the tender.
- Ensure conformity with legislation.
- Make sure that information and advice is accessible by discussing the draft specification with colleagues who might have worked on a similar project.

■ Use plain language and avoid library jargon.
■ Be realistic when specifying requirements. These should include any limits imposed, what can or cannot be tolerated, deliverables and time-scales.

A badly drawn up specification may result in:

■ failure to achieve value for money
■ the risk of disputes arising with suppliers in relation to the work and outcomes
■ not getting the right skills for the job.

Table 6.2 on the next page provides a sample list of criteria for architect selection. The selection panel would need to agree the criteria and the scale and range of points possible beforehand and then use the sheet to score each firm at the time of selection. It is important to agree these so as to be able to explain how particular candidates fared in the case of any subsequent query.

Procurement processes

It is important that the librarian makes the right decision about selecting an architect and follows agreed procedures for the recruiting and tendering processes. Depending on the value of the contract, competitive bidding can involve telephone quotations, written quotations or formal written tenders. For EU tenders, special directives apply. In all cases guidance should be sought from the organization's procurement officer, to ensure compliance. As each tender has unique features, specifications and operational requirements and tender documents should be drawn up with reference to the organization's own policy.

It is important to distinguish between tenders for services (architect–design team and other specialist consultants) and the tender for works. This is complicated as there are a number of formats that can be followed. The main options are set out in CABE's *Creating Excellent Buildings* (Section 2.6 of the first edition). They include:

Table 6.2 Criteria for architect selection and score sheet (source: RIBA, 1999)		
Categories	**Possible points**	**Points awarded**
1 Grasp of project requirements *(Client may evaluate firm's analysis, their preparation and level of interest.)*		
2 Design approach/methodology *(Client may evaluate firm or individual's creativity and problem-solving ability.)*		
3 Key personnel and roles *(Client may evaluate personal qualifications and professional skills of key individuals.)*		
4 Pertinent experience, firm *(Client may evaluate related projects presented as previous work of the firm.)*		
5 Pertinent experience, individual *(Client may evaluate related projects presented as previous work of the key personnel.)*		
6 Consultant in-house resources *(Client may evaluate firm's abilities and importance of consultant or in-house support services, training and provision of continuing professional development (CPD).)*		
7 Technical project management *(Client may evaluate firm's abilities related to technical functions such as project cost, controls, construction observation, time scheduled, etc.)*		
8 Responsiveness to client's concerns *(Client may evaluate firm's ability to form successful marketing relationships and communications with the client.)*		
9 Approach to quality *(Client may evaluate firm's methods of developing a quality project.)*		
10 Method of charging *(Client may evaluate firm's method of determining fees. Compensation statements or fee bids are not required.)*		
11 Other relevant issues *(Client may evaluate importance of other relevant issues presented by the firm.)*		
12 Reference check		

- the traditional method (architect-led team reporting directly to the client or client representative
- the managed process (where the client appoints a construction-based project manager)
- design and build (where the product is delivered for a set fee)
- various public–private schemes (some involving the client in leasing the building which may continue to be managed by the developer) (CABE, 2003).

A typical tendering process might involve:

- obtaining financial approval
- drawing up specification
- drawing up a set of quality criteria against which to evaluate architects
- advertising for interest (invite from appropriate approved list, or advertise in relevant journal)
- sending out pre-tender questionnaire
- sending out information pack
- inviting tenders
- checking references
- checking financial qualifications
- selecting those to tender
- sending out documents
- returning tenders
- evaluating tenders
- selecting preferred architect (supplier)
- post-tender negotiations
- awarding contract
- managing contract.

Summary

- Each project is unique; the architect's main function is to deliver solutions to design challenges.
- The architect has a crucial role to play and as such it is vital to get the 'right person for the job'. The ability to listen and engage with the project team may be as important as technical ability.
- Wherever possible, it is good practice to consider several architects, using clear selection criteria to determine who is best for the project. Money spent at this stage may be money well spent.
- Selection criteria might include the architect's grasp of the project requirements; the 'in-house' resources they can provide; the relevance of individual and/or the firm's experience; their approach to quality and cost.
- It is important to be aware of and follow procurement processes as required by the organization itself and/or parent organization.

Chapter 7

Partnership and community engagement

Increasingly, agencies involved in providing public services are working together. This chapter looks at the emergence of multi-agency projects and community engagement, together with some practical issues relating to dual-use libraries.

Libraries manifest a community's intellectual and cultural identity.
(Libris, http://librisdesign.org/docs/index.html)

Different types of library have different user groups. In a university or school library, the users are students and teaching staff. In a public library the users are members of the community ranging from small children to older citizens. In a special library they are members of the organization served by the library. Consideration of users is fundamental to library design, and it is therefore crucial that their views are sought through the design process.

Partnership approaches

In the 21st century there is a general expectation that service provision should be developed via a multi-agency approach in order to secure maximum efficiency and impact. Therefore, in the early stages of planning a new or refurbished library, it is wise to give some thought to how a multi-agency approach might be developed. The approach taken will depend on the philosophy of the project, the aim and purpose of the new or refurbished building, the needs of stakeholders and local opportunities.

There are many toolkits and resources available on the internet to assist the development of partnerships. The following factors have frequently been identified in effective partnership work:

■ The agencies involved have a history of working together.
■ The partnership goals address needs and issues that are relevant to all members, and add value to their own activities.
■ The roles of members are complementary, not competitive, and the ways of working are agreed by all.
■ Members support each other, with agreed mechanisms for control and mutual accountability.
■ Senior management of member organizations support the partnership.
■ Members share control and are represented and influential in decision-making processes.
■ Effective systems for communication and information sharing are developed.
■ Members have confidence that each of the others will carry out activities to a high standard.
■ Members are able to learn not only from the outputs of the partnership but also from the process itself, e.g. learning new ways of working.
■ Conflicts and problems are viewed as opportunities for learning.

Funding opportunities

A significant impetus for partnership work is that funding routes are changing, with opportunities for libraries to access funding from a wider range of sources. As neighbourhoods grow or are regenerated, so the role of the library as a community facility develops, with additional resources required to ensure that needs can be met. Sustainability is a key issue. One way of meeting the funding challenge, adopted by several local authorities, is to require contributions towards the costs of community resources (including libraries) from housing developers. To simplify and standardize this process in relation to libraries, the Museums, Libraries and Archives Council (MLA) has developed a 'public library tariff', through which a calculation is made based on a standard 30 m² per 1000 population plus an average cost per person for construction and equipment. Further information about this can be found in *The National Public Library Tariff* (Elson, 2007) and a recent update (MLA, 2008).

There are other funding opportunities that may be available to libraries at a local level; for example, in 2007, £58 million was made available for public libraries across the UK through the Big Lottery Community Libraries Fund. Regeneration funding streams are also sometimes available. In 2004 the Department of Culture, Media and Sport (DCMS) consulted widely on culture as a means of urban regeneration. In the consultation document (DCMS, 2004) reference was made to various buildings that had had an effect on their area, for example Bournemouth Public Library, described as 'a new public living room', 'a catalyst for the upgrading of the public realm in that particular area of the town' and 'not just a library, but a welcoming hub of the community' (2004, 22). Culture is seen as pivotal to the success of regenerated areas, and libraries may be able to acquire funds as part of local regeneration projects. All these sources will require evidence of partnership work and community engagement.

Consultation

> Construction of a library sends a strong message: if the city cares enough to build the library, they must care about me.
>
> (Mary Dempsey, Chicago Library Commissioner,
> cited in Barber and Wallace, 2007, 61)

Community consultation and briefings are important considerations in the planning of a new library, particularly a public library. If the proposed library is to satisfy local needs and satisfy funders that it is viable, early community consultation and data collection are essential to develop the community profile and identify community needs. The community profile will consist of:

- demographics
- employment statistics
- existing facilities
- population changes
- geography
- transport infrastructure.

Identification of community needs requires in-depth consultation with existing groups and society, and broader based engagement and dialogue with the wider community. Consultation can be carried out using a range of methods – questionnaires, open days, exhibitions, public meetings, focus groups, themed workshops and similar activities – to give the opportunity for individuals of all ages to express their opinions and concerns. It is important that all stakeholders are involved in the consultation process including, for example, the vice chancellor for a university library.

Janine Schmidt demonstrates the importance of marketing in complementing the consultation process. In the IFLA library building guidelines, she notes: 'Marketing strategies emphasise that library design starts not from collections but from the clients and the experiences they have in libraries' (Schmidt, 2007, 55). Although there is no substitute for finding out what users would like, Schmidt warns: 'Most libraries conduct user surveys but sometimes fail to translate requirements into library design specifications' (2007, 58–9).

Community engagement

Figure 7.1 shows the change in thinking in ways of engaging one's community: the move from a passive to an active seeking and sharing of views throughout the life of the project. This is the thinking behind the term 'community engagement'.

Community engagement is about involving local people in decision making, service planning and development as *equal* partners. In this way it differs from consultation, which may be *a part of* community engagement but is not the same thing; consultation provides an opportunity for people to comment on and influence ideas but does not give them an equal say in the final decision-making process. This is illustrated in Figure

7.2. In other words engagement continues throughout the project's life, whereas consultation is usually only at the pre-building stage.

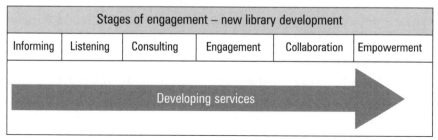

Stages of engagement – new library development					
Informing	Listening	Consulting	Engagement	Collaboration	Empowerment

Developing services

Figure 7.1 Stages of engagement

Stage 1	Stage 2	Stage 3
Project ideas	→ Design	→ Implementation
Consultation	No further involvement	
Engagement	→ → → → → → →	

Figure 7.2 Community consultation and engagement

There are many definitions of community engagement. In a library context, the following definition has been endorsed by MLA, quoting from an earlier government consultation *Your Neighbourhood: getting involved and having a say*, itself a preliminary study for Office of the Deputy Prime Minister (ODPM, 2005a):

Where community engagement is taking place, what do we want to see?
- more people everywhere getting actively involved in their neighbourhoods
- local people able to influence decisions about their own neighbourhoods and public services.

(MLA/CSV Consulting, 2006)

The MLA, in partnership with CSV Consulting, produced a toolkit for libraries to support community engagement (MLA/CSV Consulting, 2006). Community engagement can be hard work; however, the benefits can be significant. As the document states, community engagement is good for the library service because it can:

■ increase wider support among the community for the library service
■ provide services to the wider community that are not possible within existing resource constraints
■ increase the profile of the library across the authority as a department that can deliver on different agendas
■ increase library use
■ create advocates in the community
■ involve under-represented groups
■ make the services offered more reflective of community needs
■ provide an opportunity for staff development
■ encourage new groups of people to consider entering the library and information profession
■ attract funding
■ gain input from under-represented groups about service development
■ contribute to making the library a centre of the community
■ increase the extent to which the authority sees the library as a mechanism for communicating with communities.

(2006, 5)

Figure 7.3 shows the way in which community engagement works as a continuum through the building's inception and whole life, and provides examples of ways in which this is achieved.

The government in the early 21st century has endorsed its commitment to community engagement through a number of schemes for neighbourhood renewal and citizen empowerment (NAO, 2004; ODPM and Home Office, 2005). Community engagement may be a relatively new concept for libraries but it is one which has increasing importance as the government document *Framework for the Future* suggested:

Community involvement continuum				
Providing information	Gathering information	Interaction	Engaging empowerment	Community
Inform/ promote e.g. publicity to promote new library	Consult e.g. providing a questionnaire to gain views of customers on new library	Discuss/ debate e.g. discussion with stake-holders through public meetings	Engage/ participate e.g. formal arrangements – user groups actively involved in library development	Empower e.g. community takes the lead in planning and delivering the new service

Figure 7.3   Community involvement continuum

All libraries need to work to establish programmes that will engage groups and individuals that are hard to reach by identifying them and establishing what are their particular needs and then by redesigning services when necessary so that there are no barriers to inclusion. Those libraries which are already successful in this important work, frequently involve the communities themselves in the design and implementation of services.   (DCMS, 2003, 41)

A good example of community engagement in action can be found in the northwest of England. Bury Metro Libraries (2006) have developed a number of outreach libraries 'with and for local people'. In terms of engaging the community in library planning they suggest the following areas of activity are important:

- finding a locality
- meeting local people informally
- liaising with other agencies
- looking for a community partner
- consulting
- setting up a steering group
- providing library service resources
- source funding and support

- ■ assessing potential problems
- ■ drawing up a realistic plan (Bury Metro Libraries, 2006, 4).

In all of these there is a need to engage with people *where they are* in terms of providing accessible opportunities for consultation and in thinking about the location for setting up the service. Librarians will need to get the message across that libraries have changed, but they will also need to listen to the wishes of the communities who live in the places in which they are hoping to set up new facilities. There should be no sense of using 'cast-off' materials or equipment from existing libraries to start up new facilities. Most importantly, library staff must allow opportunities for the community to comment, criticize and change plans where possible. However, scope for change is related to the stage of development. Design changes made at late stages may incur more expense as the project progresses. Changes during the construction period can incur heavy penalties especially if they result in delays on site – or can be claimed to have led to such delays.

Linked to this is useful research by Barlow and Morris (2007) who have examined the usability of public libraries in comparison to bookshops. They compared ten public libraries (five old and five new) and four bookshops. Libraries were paired such that there was an old and a new one in the same locality. Through a series of way-finding and retrieval tasks, users supplied information, which was evaluated in relation to a number of objectives, notably: 'To provide insight for library designers to improve provision for new users' (Barlow and Morris, 2007, 3).

Libraries and bookshops did different things well in terms of usability, and the conclusions repay reading for those contemplating a new library project. In particular the walkthrough audit would be a useful tool in helping planners assess the potential usability of their new build.

Dual-use libraries

As approaches to planning involve a wider range of agencies and individuals, so the results of that planning may change. A joint-use (dual or multi-use) library is one in which two or more distinct groups of users are served equally in the same premises, and the service is managed co-operatively between two or more agencies. Secondary schools are the most frequent location for such services, but they may also be established by public libraries in association with other agencies, for example a community facility, children's centre or centre that includes both school and library.

There has been a lot of discussion in professional literature about the pros and cons of single versus dual-use facilities. Dual-use libraries appear on paper to have many advantages: it might be expected that better library provision would result from a joint service than from a single service. However, views are mixed, depending on good or bad experiences. Some of the potential advantages and disadvantages of dual-use libraries are listed below.

Advantages
- a single set of premises
- a single set of staff
- library materials and equipment serving two groups of users who, in other circumstances, are provided for separately
- potential interaction between the two groups (e.g. school pupils and the general public).

Disadvantages
- a site that is not central and thus a drawback for one group
- misunderstandings of the roles of the joint service
- mixed perceptions of the library's clientele
- a reluctance of staff to embrace change.

A report to the Commonwealth Schools Commission about Australian libraries (1983) suggests the following factors are significant in the experience of dual-use facilities:

Potential issues
- planning problems, such as inadequate assessment of user needs
- governance problems, for example, absence of a formal agreement and of commitment to the concept

Keys to success
- a firm commitment by the two partners to the project
- a single staffing structure
- a clear understanding by all concerned of the philosophical and operational aspects involved

- physical problems, such as difficulties of public access due to the location in community and/or school
- user problems, for example, dual systems of acquisition and use of the library as a classroom
- staffing problems, such as inadequate staffing levels and inflexible and territorial attitudes.

- a formal signed agreement before the joint service begins
- a building of adequate size for the two groups, designed to facilitate both group and individual use
- effective channels of communication and responsibility.

Although these factors go beyond the planning process, the following issues should be considered during the design phase of buildings being developed for dual use:

- *on-site location* – 'good visibility from and proximity to a thoroughfare and adjacent parking are needed'
- *access and entry* – a common entrance is preferred and the users should not have a complicated route via playground or buildings to the library
- *external lighting and signposting* – to ensure safe access identify the library building and the route to it
- *internal design and furnishing* – for example, separate accommodation, class-size group, adequate staff and storage areas, sufficient shelving and seating, bearing in mind different age groups.   (Commonwealth Schools Commission, 1983)

A wider range of institution types is now working in joint-use facilities, for example, school–community, government–university and research–business libraries.

A good example of a college–public library facility is The Bridge in Glasgow, UK. This is cited in a recent book by Sarah McNicol where she outlines the key features of this successful merger:

- The physical merging of the college and library facilities
- The transfer of college library staff to the employment of the council and college 'buy back' of library services
- The allocation of responsibility for ICT service delivery for both communities to the college
- The production of a legally binding service-level agreement
- A single library management system and catalogue
- The provision of college learning support services to both communities as part of its wider community learning partnership.   (McNicol, 2008, 9)

Partnership arrangements in joint-use facilities will need to be more formal than in other library settings. Legal agreements must be drawn up where possible to make responsibilities and boundaries clear for all parties. McNicol quotes a checklist of areas to cover (Table 7.1).

Table 7.1   Areas to cover in legal agreements for joint-use facilities
(source: McNicol, 2008, 9)

Theme	Detail
Governance	Funding arrangements, state laws and regulations
Planning	Community involvement; process for handling disputes
Staffing	Certification requirements
Facility	Accessibility, separate entrances, parking, caretaking, signage, furniture, areas for different activities – e.g. group instruction
Focus of the collection	Cataloguing, collection development policies, policies for sharing materials
Funding	Minimum levels, joint plans for capital improvements, yearly operating budget
Hours of opening	Weekends, evenings
Internet access	Dedicated PCs for adult users, joint plan for purchase and maintenance of technology

Although these points relate particularly to a school–public facility (suggested by the New Jersey Association of School Librarians), they can be usefully transferred to other joint-use settings.

A service level agreement might be drawn up between partnerships sharing a facility. This should define terms and aim to clarify:

- the scope of the agreement
- service specifications including exclusions
- operating standards and obligations, including:
  - availability and quality of service
  - provision of premises and support facilities
  - performance monitoring
  - management procedures
  - business continuity
  - sustainability and residual costs.

Summary

- Partnership approaches are increasingly being used, for various reasons, not least because they enable a more effective use of resources and the ability to make joint funding bids.
- Community engagement is relatively new to libraries but seems set to stay. It involves engaging with local people and agencies as equal partners. This is more than consultation because it continues over the full life of the project.
- Dual-use facilities have advantages and drawbacks; the appropriateness of this approach will be determined by the philosophy of the service and aims of the project. Those embarking on dual-use projects will need to draw up legally binding working agreements.

Chapter 8

The design brief*

The design brief is the statement of requirements on which the design is developed. The brief may start as a simple general statement of the project objectives; the 'outline' brief. This should provide the basic information required by the architect, but architects will themselves take part in the planning process, creating a detailed brief that will equip them to create the design. This chapter explores the contents of the design brief and the processes involved in creating it, drawing on documents used in actual new library builds as well as technical literature.

Functions of the brief

A good brief is vital – one should never start design work until the operational brief is established and space requirements and key relationships have been set out. The design brief can be useful in many ways. Architects generally agree that the brief can provide:

■ a channel of information between librarian and architect
■ a basis for discussion and joint problem-solving

- a record of decisions and milestones; this can support continuity and consistency of the project's development
- a useful evaluation tool, as it includes aims and resources against which designs can be evaluated
- a useful aid for estimating resources required.

The design brief may also be part of the legal agreement between librarian and architect.

Although it is possible to have a verbal brief, a written brief provides a clear source of reference for all involved. Developing the brief is the most important part of the whole scheme; however magnificent an architect's creation, however skilful she/he may be in solving a problem, the solution is useless if the problem's true nature and extent has not been understood. In most if not all cases, therefore, the brief should be written to ensure that there is a common understanding about what is required. The librarian is responsible for seeing that the brief describes clearly what she/he would like the project to accomplish, for reviewing and signing it off at outline and detailed stages. The architect's team is entitled to have a document which will be their authority to spend valuable time in working in a certain direction.

Core elements

At its most basic, the design brief can be divided into three elements:

- *statement of the purpose* the library is to serve and the place it is to occupy within the social, educational or commercial framework: the library's relationship to the other institutions, departments or sections of its environment
- *detailed record* of the library's exact requirements as an operational unit, including quantities of books and other materials to be accommodated, the readers and users to be served, their needs and the opening times at which these will be met, staff to be housed, and the physical relationship between these different elements

■ *record of the limitations* imposed by the authority or institution: the chosen site, any known height or access restrictions together with the financial and other controls which have been determined.

In a straightforward project these three elements may be quite brief. In any large scheme, however, it is better for them to be detailed so that consultation can then take place on each section, as questions arise in the minds of the architect and/or the library team.

The brief should be consistent within itself, and with any other related projects (whether or not for buildings). It should also be realistic in terms of aims, resources, context and quality to be achieved. Although some background information may help the architect to understand the context, the brief should focus on information and decisions directly relevant to the project. Background information that is provided should be clearly organized to support, not obscure, important information about needs.

Outcome-based approach

The best approach to writing a brief is to define as clearly as possible the desired outcomes for the project; it is then the role of the inventive design team and architect to specify design solutions to achieve the outcomes. In a private finance initiative (PFI*) scheme, the brief, in the form of an 'output specification', aims to ensure that the risk of achieving the outcome is transferred to the provider.

Priorities should be established for the aims of the project. It should be possible to classify items in the brief as 'essential', 'desirable' or 'would like'. The architect needs to know about:

■ the degree of importance of particular items
■ any 'critical' aspects of the project – those that will cause the project to fail if not fulfilled
■ any uncertainties or difficulties the library team experienced in formulating the brief.

This information will help the architect understand the extent to which she/he is free to be creative in the design of the library, and what is negotiable and what is not in relation to the output specifications.

The brief is a starting point for the dialogue between the librarian and architect. Therefore, it should be specific enough for decisions and actions to be taken but flexible enough to encourage exploration of problems, options and uncertainties. However, at some point, the architects will 'freeze' the brief so that they can work on the designs and form of the building, and cost estimates produced.

Stages of development

The development of the brief, incorporating the elements above, will take the project from a vision to a detailed building manual. The librarian must sign off the brief at critical stages.

The vision statement and business plan prepare the background, and are followed by the outline brief. This is developed in discussion with the architect to produce the detailed brief. When finally agreed, this forms the basis of the design work, which, when completed, provides the information for the architect to prepare working drawings and the quantity surveyor to draw up the detailed specification. The contractor can prepare the tender for the work and then proceed to build in accordance with the agreed design.

The building manual records how everything works and is handed over to the client at the end of the process so that she/he understands how to run and maintain the completed building.

Figure 8.1 shows a logical sequence of activity relating to the design process (further details in Eley, 2003).

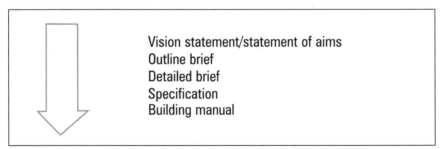

Figure 8.1   The written design process

Statement of aims

The terms of the statement within the design brief will be different from those used when the librarian presented a case for creating a new library to his or her authority or institution. Rather than generalizations on the cultural, social or economic advantages to the community, this statement should confine itself to a definition of objectives, both immediate and long term. In order to do this it may be necessary to explain the programme and objectives of the parent institution itself.

Perhaps the most difficult part of the brief to write, this statement has to express clearly and concisely the role of the library in the life of the community or of the parent organization. This may be very different to traditional expectations about libraries; for example:

■ A modern public library often incorporates, or complements, other services in a way that is very different from the traditional perceptions of libraries. The architect needs to understand the relationships and requirements they bring to the project.

■ In a school, the library's contribution depends on the educational methods to be used. In the traditional pattern the school library was a place where books were kept and where children went to read them at certain hours. Today, in increasing numbers of schools, the library is a dynamic centre, which exploits media of many different kinds and which is continually in use, with contacts in both directions from each element of teaching and learning. Unless the architect knows this they can hardly design a framework appropriate for the proposed activity.

■ A library in a hospital may be planned to serve the recreational needs of the patients, or of a certain section of the patients, the medical staff, the technical staff, the professional and recreational needs of the nurses, or any combinations of these. The architect must know exactly which apply in a particular case.

From the statement, the architect needs to be able both to gain an understanding of the library as an operational unit and to visualize the environmental conditions which must be created to meet the aims.

The outline brief

The outline brief develops the vision or statement into a more detailed statement of user requirements, incorporating the views of all the key stakeholders, including future users; it should make reference to accommodation, function and standards. The librarian must ensure that, through the outline brief, the architect has a clear picture of the library vision. If any of it is left to guesswork on the architect's part, the result may be unsuitable. However, a good brief will also be allowed to evolve during the early stages. In its final form, the brief should not seek to prescribe how to meet the project's objectives; that is the work of the design team. It should capture:

- the wider vision
- the specific activities and operational requirements
- the desired image, atmosphere and quality
- criteria for site selection where appropriate.

If teamwork is already in process, the development of the outline brief will have been preceded by general discussions within the team, which will ensure a sympathetic reception. In the case of simple designs which might be repeated in the future (for example, a series of small branch libraries), the architect could produce some preliminary design ideas, which might be used as a basis for team discussion leading to the production of a jointly prepared definitive brief.

The main aim of the outline brief is to provide the architect with a description of the challenge for which solutions are needed in terms of space and organization. However, the process of creating the brief forces the library team to focus their own thinking and to examine the organization and methods of the proposed library. It is essential that everyone is clear about how the new library is to operate, both generally and in detail, and that the brief reflects this. If not, the end result is almost certainly going to be unsatisfactory.

The biggest challenge that planners and the design team face is to arrive at a balance between what may be contradictory goals, that is, to balance conflicting priorities so that the building can realize as many of the goals as possible. Nolan Lushington lists some key objectives in his practical guide on library design for users (Lushington, 2002, 16). Some of these are incorporated in the following list of goals and outcomes for a library building which might be included in a typical brief. It should:

- be located in a situation that is both convenient and prominent
- provide for the convenience of the library's users (and potential users) while maximizing staff efficiency
- provide a modern library with up-to-date technologies that reflect the cultural make-up of the community
- provide a comfortable and inviting ambience that encourages use but allows staff to maintain control and supervision and allow out-of-hours use
- provide a reference and seating area that invites users to approach librarians but provides the option for private consultation
- provide efficient staff and technical service work areas to assure good productivity
- provide an attractive, efficient design for current needs while leaving open the potential for future expansion and change
- provide multi-purpose rooms that can be supervised when the library is open, and be accessible when the rest of the library is closed
- have efficient material circulation design for convenient public service and self-service
- be fully accessible for people with disabilities and users with buggies
- provide natural light to flood the library but control excessive heat gain from direct sunlight to minimize damage to materials and control energy costs
- provide plentiful artificial light without glare
- provide heating, ventilation and air conditioning (HVAC*), and electrical systems for future expansion, and for increased occupancy.
- provide operable windows for between-season ventilation or air conditioning
- be flexible to allow for future expansion for specific functions such as children's services, teen youth services, book stacks and electronic workstations.

A good architect will probe and question the brief to find the best way to meet the librarian's needs. While the librarian and their team may be able to write the first version, it is advisable to get independent expert advice from someone with design experience to take it to a level from which a final design can be created. This person is sometimes referred to as a client adviser.

The detailed brief

Once the objectives have been stated, the context for the new service has been set but not the solution. The next step is to develop the outline brief in more detail and consider feasibility options for the realization of the objectives. This will require the expertise of external consultants and architects. The final design plan will be based on the feasibility study, setting out a number of options which can be compared. To get to that stage, the brief will need to:

- define the options
- gather information
- assess and analyse the options.

Define the options

A basic comparison can be made between the future needs of the library and the ability of the current premises to support them. A feasibility study can then be carried out by building professionals to look at various ways to meet the objectives. These might include:

- a 'do nothing' option, to highlight how the current accommodation would cope with future scenarios
- options that reorganize the existing building fabric, with different levels of replacement (and disruption)
- a total or substantially new build option.

Gather information

This should be done for each of the options. Information about all of the options should be obtained in relation to their relative advantages, likely disruption to the service, and longer-term maintenance implications. It is also crucial that the estimated cost of each option is compared, in terms of both the initial capital cost and the 'whole life' cost over at least 25 years. In estimating costs it is important to recognize that:

- a clear definition of what the budget includes is *essential* – the building and site, consultants' fees and expenses through to completion, taxes, equipping the building, access roads, move costs for the library and its collections, etc.; costs should also include temporary rehousing of library services if necessary, furniture and equipment (both fixed and loose), and landscaping
- early cost estimates can only be based on broad assumptions, such as expected cost per square metre of floor area; in a few cases a fixed price contract will provide cost commitment early on; financial consequences of the main project decisions should be estimated as the decisions are made; if postponed, costs can go out of control
- the potential impact of inflation; e.g. in a large library building due to open five to eight years from the date of the brief, the costs would be considerably higher once inflation is taken into account. Those involved will need to agree how this will be accounted for in the cost estimates.

The brief and design need to be fairly firm before detailed cost estimates can be made. They must take into account, for example, the degree of flexibility of the building and its expected life in relation to quality. Also, as the project progresses, any officers communicating with the media must make it clear which costs are current or projected to the planned construction phase.

Assess and analyse the options

Scoring and weighting can be applied by setting out the options against the objectives in a table, combining financial and non-financial factors to produce a best-value solution. When the preferred option is chosen, it should provide a feasibility design that incorporates the library's vision of the future.

Flexibility and adaptability

Flexibility and adaptability are essential in the brief for any project: It is important to be clear what needs to be adaptable (for instance, internal walls being able to be removed and rebuilt without affecting the structure or major services) and what should be flexible for more frequent change. For instance, sliding or folding doors can often be underused and ineffective, but may provide flexibility in allowing spaces to change size to match changing needs (for example, by offering additional study spaces during examination months).

The flexibility to allow for change must be a key design requirement. Whatever layout is preferred, it must be flexible to allow for future changes, for instance for different usage. What is suitable now may well need to be changed in a few years. Flexibility also allows for daily change of use, such as accommodating author visits and events through movable furniture and portable ICT. Avoiding fixed furniture and limiting the range allows flexibility. Multi-functional furniture can also provide flexibility, although this must be offset with the need for simple products, which are not difficult to repair or replace.

Adaptability is needed to allow for longer-term changes such as developments in subject collections, implications of evolving ICT. The consequences for the library if the design does not allow for adaptability can be significant.

Amending the brief

Most libraries are now created as part of larger organizations, and library design may be utterly dependent on the change and development of those organizations. However, amending the design brief can be an expensive luxury and should never be used as a substitute for forethought.

After the completed outline brief has been sent to the architect, the librarian should, as far as is humanly possible, comply with it. Inevitably changes may be made, but they should arise from changed circumstances, not from changed ideas. The time for the librarian to think hard is before writing the brief, not afterwards. Any necessary changes must be notified, in writing, to the architect as soon as possible: all changes cost time and money, but the later in the scheme they occur, the more expensive they become. At a certain point, usually before detailed design begins, the architect is entitled to impose a freeze date; a point beyond which no changes in the brief should be made; changes after that date may be possible but they will be very expensive indeed.

It should be noted here that the contractor will assess any areas where claims might be made for further funds from the client (see 'Claims' in Appendix 1). This is an area where disputes can occur and, even where not justified, can add to the costs (because the client decides that it is cheaper to pay than to go through the arbitration process).

Summary

■ The main purpose of the design brief is to provide a clear statement about the project requirements, to inform the architect's design. However, it also serves as a useful tool for ensuring the librarian is clear about what is required.

■ The brief provides a clear point of reference throughout the project, for architect and librarian.

■ The brief has three core elements: statement of aims, a detailed record of requirements and a record of limitations.

■ The outline brief develops the vision or statement of aims into a more detailed statement of requirements, in response to which the architect can start to propose solutions.

■ The detailed brief builds on the outline and usually includes a feasibility study, an analysis of the various options and costings.

■ It is important to build flexibility and adaptability into the design requirements.

■ Although the brief will be subject to many changes there will come a point at which the architect can ask for a 'freeze'. Any changes made after this point could prove very costly – during or after RIBA Work Stage D, post planning application stage.

Chapter 9

Design quality

> The design of library buildings should be addressed at three levels: urban design, building design and interior design. Each has specific requirements which involve dialogue with user and interest groups, and each level has its own exacting demands which cannot be overlooked. This chapter explores the different elements of design quality.

Urban design

In pointing out the importance of good urban design CABE sets out to define what that entails: 'By good design we mean design that is fit for purpose, sustainable, efficient, coherent, flexible, responsive to context, good looking and a clear expression of the requirements of the brief' (CABE, 2006b, 5).

Those who are planning and designing a new public library need to bear in mind its place as a civic building, while academic libraries need to be at the hub of college or university activity. In addition to supporting their ever developing collections and needs, it is essential that libraries are close to pedestrian traffic and public transport. The external library space should be free of cars but there needs to be provision for disabled access and facilities for the storage of bicycles.

Most libraries will have a public 'front' and a service entrance, the latter often at the rear or underneath the building. The public entrance is often a space where users gather together immediately in front of or outside the door itself. It should be a place where users can meet, chat and take short breaks. Therefore it can be helpful to design it in a similar way to a public mall, with attention to landscape design, seating and personal safety.

The entrance doors themselves need to be wide and transparent; as soon as they arrive, users should be able to see, and feel invited into, the interior of the library. It should also be possible to view the major library spaces from the outside; too frequently the demands for security interrupt the physical and visible flows between the inside and outside worlds.

Life expectancy of different functions of the building

Buildings are comparatively permanent, while the organization and activities within them are continuously changing. 'Shell and core' describe the building envelope, its structure and 'skin' (walls and columns), and its servicing elements (stairs, lifts, lavatories, lobbies, ducts and plant rooms). The 'scenery' refers to components such as ceilings, lighting and finishes. Settings (furniture and equipment) are the things that can be easily moved as necessary to meet changing needs. Table 9.1 summarizes the typical life expectancy of different functions of the building.

Table 9.1 Life expectancy of different functions of the building	
Element	Length of time
Site	Indefinite
Structure	80 years
Skin	50–70 years
Services	15–20 years
Scenery	7–8 years
Settings	Daily

Factors that affect the planning and form of a building include type of client, location, site condition, planning restriction, access, long- and short-term use of buildings, organizational change, required image, management, maintenance, budget and programme. The library project needs to take into account elements of the above, which all last for different lengths of time. It is important to discuss this with the architect and specify the life of the building. Obviously this will have a bearing on the cost of the project. It is very unusual to have a building specified as lasting over 100 years.

Site selection

Site selection may be a foregone conclusion where a project is part of a wider development, for example, in a school or university. If, however, the librarian is consulted about the choice of site, there are several factors that should be considered. These include the availability of land and its acquisition, ground conditions, accessibility, climate and legal issues such as approval for use and construction. Each of these factors will affect a library's real and perceived success when measured in terms of the quality of design, construction costs, meeting the budget and building schedule.

The physical impact of the library building and of its surrounding landscape is important, both from a distance and in the approach to the building. The quality of space, sounds and light inside the building are also crucial considerations for its design.

Designers need to put the building into the context of its surrounding environment. It may thereby enhance the local environment and add value to the neighbourhood. They will also need to consider the impact of the building on its surroundings, in terms of its size, style and the construction materials. All these will have an impact on neighbouring buildings, routes to the site and views. The design team may wish to use the BREEAM assessment tools. These are designed to help construction professionals understand and mitigate the environmental impacts of the developments they design and build (see www.breeam.org/index.jsp).

Ideally, the library should be as close as possible to the heart of the community it serves, near other facilities and accessible by public transport (particularly for a public library). A flat site is preferable because the construction costs are lower than with sloping plots, and it allows for easier access. It should have adequate space for delivery, disabled parking and bicycles. The profile of the local community is an important consideration, as the library will need to meet their needs and aspirations. Consideration will need to be given to the choice between a single-storey or a multi-storey building. A single-storey building is generally preferable because of a range of factors, such as staffing, access and security.

If the librarian has the opportunity to contribute to the selection of a site, as suggested by Lushington (2002, 73-4), the following basic criteria should be considered:

- *Access* - A site that encourages people to use the library is most important. In a public library setting this might mean choice of a site that users will pass when going to work or shopping. The site should be considered as a centre of population and in the context of its nearness to other civic or institutional amenities.
- *Location* - This needs to be satisfactory and acceptable to the population being served.
- *Traffic flow* (ingress and egress) and traffic controls - Accessibility by public transport and for car users needs to be considered.
- *Site availability* - The site needs to be available for immediate use/purchase. If there are conditions such as buried fuel tanks or other environmental hazards, these need to be worked into the plan, as do constraints on historic buildings. It is important to evaluate any development limits that affect a potential new build, for example, maximum area, height restrictions.
- *Topography* - This includes any site grading needs for preparation of the site and other natural features that might affect the development.
- *Solar and wind orientation* - Local solar and wind patterns are important. Much of the energy demand in buildings is for light and climate control. The site should allow for maximum use of natural light and ventilation. The effect of the sun's glare on the building for all users will need to be assessed.
- *Visibility* - The site should be in a prominent position, and have natural views to and from the site. It should be quickly and conveniently accessible.
- *User and staff safety* - The site will need to be safe and secure at night and well lit. Parking should be accessible nearby and child safety

considered in terms of proximity to major roads.

- *Community synergy* - It is crucial to check the proximity of other community amenities, perhaps as part of a cultural quarter or retail area. Included in this should be the current known footfall in the area.
- *Size for growth* - The site needs to be considered in terms of its ability to accommodate expanded library facilities if required in the future. This might include extension to the building and facilities such as parking.
- *Cost factors* - The site needs to minimize costs involved. Purchase price, site clearance and development costs all need to be considered.
- *Infrastructure* - It is important to estimate the extent of new or modified infrastructure needs, e.g. water, power, re-routing of utilities.
- *Other considerations* - There will be unique factors based on the local context and political climate, e.g. regeneration potential.

It is useful to assign a point value to each site (perhaps a score of 0–5) depending on the criteria. If some criteria are more important than others, the points can be weighted accordingly. For example, site size can be an important decision factor because larger sites allow more design flexibility including a buffer around the perimeter of the building.

The grid in Table 9.2 on the next page can be used as a checklist. Subsets can be made for each of the headings.

Building design

The aim of library design should be for the user to have a sense of the key areas and ways through the building from the entrance. Any security desk should be designed to channel users through while not giving the appearance of a barrier. The issue and return counters are likely to be a part of the entrance but should not dominate it. An inner entrance space is useful in softening the effect of control areas. It may be possible to use this space for information boards, meeting rooms or a café. The difficulty is creating a balance between what may be seen as 'non-library' activities and the will to show users and funders that these are all an essential part of the library experience.

Economic planning is necessary to keep costs down, so all opportunities

Table 9.2 Site evaluation criteria			
Criteria	Site A	Site B	Site C
Access			
Location			
Traffic flow			
Site availability			
Topography			
Solar and wind orientation			
Visibility			
User and staff safety			
Community synergy			
Size for growth			
Cost factors			
Infrastructure			
Other considerations			

should be taken to minimize corridors and make space useable for more than one function; e.g. central circulation space could double up as a café or informal meeting area. Circulation space must be easily monitored and have robust and hard-wearing surface finishes. Vertical circulation in multi-storey buildings must be visible and have good sight lines.

The circulation (issue and return) areas will often be the main places where staff interact with users. There must be clear signage (as well as spoken communication) to help users find their way through the library. Somewhere there will be access to the computerized catalogue and/or the ICT support area. In some libraries users may feel threatened by digital information systems, so it would still be advisable to have some kind of browsing area as part of this, perhaps with magazines or newspapers on hand.

Academic libraries tend towards two main arrangements of the book collection. The first is to stack the books near the centre of the library, arranging reading tables around the edge where there is good access to natural light and external views. The second is to place the books around the perimeter with a large central reading room, usually lit from above. In either of these, the integration of print and electronic media is now the way forward to best serve users. However, the specific requirements of computers and the nature of some paper-based collections, such as old newspapers or photographs, may mean that some collections have to be housed in special study areas for that particular type of material.

The key to storage of materials nowadays is flexibility. The building must be able to change over time without compromising the original architectural concept of the 'library'. For example, built-in furniture should be avoided, along with fixed lighting. Small rooms with load-bearing walls will be less adaptable than larger spaces that can be divided temporarily. Flexibility must not, however, be at the price of character or civic or institutional identity. This is always a fine line to tread. In a recent IFLA publication, the editor, Andrew McDonald (2007, 14), identifies ten qualities of library space:

■ functional
■ adaptable
■ accessible
■ varied
■ interactive
■ conducive
■ environmentally suitable
■ safe and secure
■ efficient
■ suitable for information technology.

These can be summed up in five key features:

■ visible, recognizable and legible as a type
■ adaptable to new information technology and physically extendable
■ comfortable and disabled friendly
■ inviting, safe and secure for users
■ secure and protecting the collection.

CABE (2006a) has identified good design as a mix of the following attributes:

■ *functionality in use*, or fitness for purpose, which can be checked against the criteria in the brief

- *build quality*, including the need for whole-life cost principles to be used
- *efficiency and sustainability*, ensuring the design allows buildings to be delivered on time and on cost
- *designing in context*, including the site and existing buildings, but also the need for the total design to be seen as a coherent whole
- *aesthetic quality*, and the need for a non-institutional, individual character.

CABE (2006a, 23) also refers to the design quality indicator (DQI) which offers a checklist under three headings:

- impact – character and innovation, forms and materials, internal environment, and urban and social integration
- build quality – performance engineering systems and construction
- functionality – use, access and space.

                                    (CABE and Resource, 2003, 26; www.dqi.org.uk)

CABE's *Design Review* begins: 'The appearance of our built environment is important, but good design is about much more than how things look. It is about uplifting communities and transforming how people feel and behave. It is also about using resources effectively and imaginatively. In short every good design improves the quality of life for everyone' (CABE, 2006b, 5).

In 2003 Bryson, Usherwood and Proctor researched the role of libraries as places, looking at the impact of new buildings, specifically the Norwich and Norfolk Millennium Library and the London Borough of Newham's Stratford Library. They noted a series of characteristics defined by earlier writers, notably Faulkner-Brown's 'Ten Commandments' and Fred Schilpf and John Moorman's 'seven deadly sins of public library architecture':

Ten commandments	Seven deadly sins
1 Flexible	1 Bad lighting
2 Compact	2 Inflexibility
3 Accessible	3 Bad location
4 Extendible	4 Complex maintenance
5 Varied	5 Insufficient work and storage space

6   Organized
7   Comfortable
8   Constant in environment
9   Secure
10 Economic.
        (Faulkner-Brown, 1999)

6   Bad security
7   Signature architecture.
        (Schilpf & Moorman, 1998)

Good design is essential for every library development, however modest, and the users' experience inside must match their expectations from the outside. Good design is not a costly luxury. In fact, best practice in integrating design and construction delivers better value for money – as well as better buildings. This is especially apparent when the full costs of a building over its lifetime are considered. Library design must also take account of financial management including cost analysis. Potential budget restrictions in the future need to be considered in relation to their impact on the design plans. It is also important formally to manage the change for staff and to plan for keeping momentum going once the building has opened.

The new project may also create opportunities to implement new initiatives such as floorwalkers, radio frequency identification (RFID*) or integrated stock. However, the librarian must look at each project afresh in order to assess current and potential need and not rely on repeating previous projects. The librarian should always aim for the best and question every process.

In 2000 the British Prime Minister set up the Better Public Building Initiative (see Appendix 2, Websites) to work towards a fundamental change in the quality of building design in the public sector. The initiative underscores the benefits of well designed public buildings: 'Good design in the public sector enhances the environment and the community, revitalizes cities and neighbourhoods, results in buildings that work well and retain a human dimension, and makes the delivery of services easier and more efficient. Design also reflects the ambitions and spirit of the people behind it' (www.betterpublicbuildings.gov.uk/about/).

Design criteria

Philippa Harper (2006, 37) cites CABE's criteria for excellence in design of public spaces:

- a welcoming, accessible building, encouraging existing and new users to cross the threshold and engage with activities in it
- a clearly identifiable entrance
- an easily navigable building organization with the ability to find one's way around building with minimal reliance on signs
- consideration of cross-flows in entrance or ticketing area, avoiding queues blocking circulation routes
- a positive contribution to the public realm . . . using social spaces such as café/bar or foyers to interface with the public realm
- meeting comfort expectations of the audience base
- contributing to vitality and viability of town centres and night-time economy
- a strong daytime and night-time presence
- a good functional fit with the specific technical requirements of the particular leisure or arts use(s)
- an attractive destination.

It is worth noting the factors that were considered by the judging panel of the Public Library Buildings Awards 2007 (McDermott, 2007). These include terms like inspiring space, user impact, tone, inclusive environments, durability, value for money, community engagement and sustainability. There is also a generic 'X factor' covering more elusive factors like the effect of the building ('wow' factor), atmosphere, attention to detail, 'a library worthy of the public'. Such elements are hard to prescribe in a design brief, but may be key to a building's prospects as an award winner.

Environmental considerations

In today's climate ever increasing energy costs will have a negative effect on running costs in the longer term. There is a preference nowadays towards the use of natural light and ventilation where possible, particularly in reader areas. However, issues around security and depth of the building can make this difficult to achieve. Generally libraries have a 'mixed-mode' ventilation system, that is, a mixture of natural and mechanical systems. Such systems may incorporate open spaces (atria) or wind turbines, for example. Solar heat gain can be a problem where there are large areas of glazing, particularly on south-facing elevations. If it is not possible to avoid glazing on south-facing walls, it may be worth investigating the provision of solar screening or special glass rather than choosing solid walls.

Low-energy light fittings and sensors should always be fitted. Task lighting can give lower general light levels. This may not be a good idea because it reduces overall light levels and can increase the risk of accidents for those with a visual impairment. The effect of light reflection on computer screens needs to be assessed. Computers may need to be sited in more central areas.

In order to maximize natural light and ventilation, the plan depth should not exceed 15 metres. However, this is difficult to achieve in all but the smallest of libraries, and hence artificial light is used in most areas. Since most libraries are constructed in urban centres, the main environmental factors are normally external air and noise pollution. Hence a great deal of attention should be directed to site choice and layout, the design of external facades and the way internal areas are created. For example, by placing book stacks against noisy external walls a more satisfactory level of comfort could be provided internally.

As a general rule, readers like to work in natural light. This normally results in the study tables being placed round the edge. Some seating areas can also be provided in inner sunlit spaces, particularly where magazines and newspapers are read. The creation of relaxation areas as distinct from study areas should take into account the different environmental conditions. The following checklist (adapted from Edwards with Khan, 2008) summarizes some options to be considered:

■ Restrict plan depth to 15 metres for maximum daylight penetration.
■ Create internal atria in large-depth libraries.
■ Provide solar shading and internal blinds on large south-facing glazing areas.
■ Use external light to increase daylight penetration.

- Place reader tables in well lit areas.
- Avoid air-conditioning if possible, because of environmental considerations, except in 'hot spots'.
- Employ mixed-mode ventilation systems.
- Maximize natural ventilation in public areas.

Increasingly, climate change will also impact on the design and planning of new library buildings, and this will need to be borne in mind from the outset of the project.

Security

It is useful to consider aspects of security in the project, as these may affect the quality of the design. Security issues will relate to the fabric of the building, the safety of collections and other resources like cash, and the safety of personnel, both users and staff. Existing policies relating to disaster management and safe handling of materials and resources will need to be adhered to. A useful starting point for consideration of all aspects of security in libraries is the manual produced by MLA (Resource, 2003).

Interior design

IFLA's recent guidelines on library building include a thorough chapter on interior design in relation to the design brief. This takes the reader through issues from creating a vision, co-operative working, assessing user needs, quantifying and qualifying the requirements of the space, defining the layout and signage, with the emphasis on the latter being 'less is more'. The chapter would repay detailed study by those charged with the interior design of a new library (Kugler, 2007).

Although paper and electronic sources are ideally brought together in one place, in reality the technical demands and characteristics of different types of media result in separate areas being allocated for each. There is usually an area for computer users, a separate area for those referring to journals or newspapers, and, in a large or academic library, a library book stack and collections of reading desks and special study carrels. Public libraries usually have a children's area, activity space, teen area, local studies collection, reference section and tourist information. The separate areas may be distinctive functional areas but they are generally linked physically and perceptually. Division of space in this way allows one area to adopt a different policy on noise or security than another, it permits internal change without disruption to the whole, and it allows different users to employ the library resources in different ways.

It is important to allow variety within the whole space. This can be engineered or left to grow as the nature of users and the collection changes. At Peckham Library in south London there are three pods within the main book areas designed specifically to house the special collections. Each is specific to the collection and tailored to the tastes of potential users.

Dividing the interior of the library into distinctive areas rather than separate rooms is the policy generally adopted in all but national libraries. Here there may be inherent conservation and security issues which require a different approach. Whatever the layout, there needs to be space for study of the library's material. Key questions to address in relation to interior design are listed below.

Technical considerations:
- Are the floor loadings adequate for the collection?
- Is the wiring layout suitable for future ICT needs?
- Are the environmental conditions acceptable for the planned use?
- Is the collection secure from fire or theft?

Aesthetic considerations:
- Is the building welcoming as well as functional?
- Are the routes and major spaces legible to the user?
- Is there space for reflection?
- Do readers have good access to daylight?

Although technical considerations such as floor loading may be the responsibility of the design team, it is useful for the librarian to be aware of them alongside the aesthetic considerations.

Ambience

Appendix 2 provides a checklist of items for discussion between librarian and architect about the ambience of the proposed library. This is not an exhaustive or comprehensive list, but more of a set of prompts for an initial discussion about the various uses of a modern library.

Fixtures and fittings

Although 'fixtures and fittings' may be left till a later stage, it is best to include them in the brief, and, most importantly, to allow an appropriate budget within the funding as a whole.

Much has changed in recent years in the design of library interiors, showing the influence of the retail sector, of the incorporation of new technology into the fabric of library buildings and in societal changes from the view of a library as a civic and, by connotation, imposing institution, to a welcoming hub of community activity.

Recent research in the retail sector has shown that consumers need 60% of any floor space to browse comfortably. So 40% should be available for fixtures and fittings. This is a fundamental point – many libraries allocate space wrongly – they have too many shelves and too much furniture, which restricts space for customers to browse. There is more information about space allocation in Chapter 10.

The rationale for the new facility should already have been decided, and there should also have been wide consultation with the user community (including potential users). This information should help the librarian to find new ways of presenting the service or help to confirm the reasons for continuing to do it in the way it has traditionally been offered. No way is the only right one, but the librarian may need to give reasons why a particular course of action has been taken.

Aesthetic as well as functional concerns mean that furniture selection is one of the most important aspects of the interior design of a library. The furnishings selected for a library should reflect the overall interior design concept of the building, while serving the functional needs of staff and users. It is important to provide a sufficiently wide variety of seating for each user to be able to satisfy personal preferences.

In small projects with no interior designer, the library staff or board sometimes select the furnishings. In these projects, the standard supplies of library or commercial furniture manufacturers are usually selected. In large, well funded projects, some of the furnishings are standard commercial items, while others are designed by architects or interior designers specifically for that library.

A number of factors affect the cost of purchasing particular furnishings. The price of an item is determined by the volume of items to be purchased; the cost of materials, labour and finishes; and competition in the marketplace. The larger the quantity of any one kind of item purchased, the lower the price of each item.

Furniture items used in libraries and other commercial settings are designed to withstand heavy use. The joinery, materials and hardware are engineered to work together to provide a durable product. Furniture is without doubt one of the most important factors in an efficient and effective modern library and as a result needs to be functional, attractive and flexible.

Certain aspects of interior design and furnishing need to be considered in the context of the project in hand, whatever its size or clientele. These are listed in Table 9.3.

Table 9.3 Furnishing considerations	
Issue system	Check-in and check-out
	Self-issue and radio frequency identification*
	Tagging and security systems
	Mechanisms for cash transactions
Shelving	Regular, display, stack, staff areas
Furniture	Tables, chairs, comfortable seating
Children's furniture	Kinderboxes, for homework, for activities
ICT provision	Public, circulation and enquiries, staff only
Designated areas	Children's, young people's, families
Study provision	Study carrels, ICT use
Specialist stock provision	Large print, audiovisual, other languages
	Reference, short-term loan
	Local interest

Each of these invites detailed consideration of the philosophy of the service and the needs of the community to be served. Many needs may appear to conflict, for example:

study   vs.   storytime
privacy   vs.   safety
access   vs.   security.

It is important to think creatively about reconciling apparently conflicting needs, most obviously through use of different zones or timing of events. Alternatives to traditional library issue or enquiry desks should always be considered, for example, 'pod'-style desks, which avoid a barrier between customer and staff.

Seemingly simple considerations like the height of shelving or the type of seating are crucial to how the library will appear to people walking through the door, and this is vital to the image the librarian wishes to project to the community. High shelves will be imposing in any setting and may actually threaten safety in small facilities where staff numbers are low.

Book stacks

Most libraries are sub-divided by book stacks which provide the basis for zoning areas into functional parts. The stacks also provide acoustic protection, have important environmental qualities (they provide thermal mass) and help define routes through the library. The position and type of shelving is essential to the smooth operation of a library and needs to be located carefully in relation to the fixed parts such as columns, lifts, stairs, walls and doors. The book stacks also dictate the layout of seating, tables and the position of workstations. Designers need to consider environmental conditions for rare books, which will affect the design of some book stack and other storage areas. Considerations for the layout of book stacks are listed in Table 9.4 (adapted from Edwards with Khan, 2008).

Table 9.4 Considerations for the layout of book stacks	
Considerations for layout of book stacks	**Secondary issues**
Position book stacks to define routes through library	Ensure safety exits are visible
Use book stacks as acoustic barriers	Consider acoustic and thermal properties of book stacks together
Compress stacks to create reader areas at perimeter of building	Provide adequate space for safe use in dense stack areas
Provide light sensors in deep stack areas	In large libraries lighting is the major energy user
Ensure floor loadings are adequate for dense book stacks	Changing internal layout can be constrained by structural limitations

ICT facilities

Growth in ICT provision is sometimes at the cost of areas for book storage. As a result shelving is often closely spaced and, increasingly, parts of the book collection are stored elsewhere. Increasing library use is sometimes achieved at the expense of space standards, both in seating areas and library shelving. Designers need to consider the needs of both readers and staff who have the task of servicing the collection. Although books are generally decreasing in size, some reference books, like art books, are larger, and currently personal computers are being used less because of an increase in ownership of laptop computers. The number of readers arriving armed with the latest digital technology, which they wish to use in the library, is increasing rapidly. Hence, layouts and service points need to accommodate these changes.

Academic libraries provide much more computer space than public libraries. In some university libraries the area given over to the ICT-based learning resource centre can exceed that of book and journal storage. The use and loan of CDs and the development of a learning rather than teaching culture have led also to the academic library being extensively employed in group teaching. Rooms are set aside for seminars within the library itself, and often the internet is the main information resource for students. This has changed the nature of most libraries from silent to quiet study areas, in many cases to spaces with a buzz of conversation and lively children's activities going on. The use of the library for seminar-type teaching also puts pressure on the lifts, stairs and corridors at the end of timetabled teaching and this can disrupt private study areas.

Many libraries are now using large plasma or LCD screens for the purpose of way-finding. These are flexible as the content can easily be changed. Considerations for the layout and design of library furniture are listed in Table 9.5 (adapted from Edwards with Khan, 2008).

Table 9.5 Considerations for the layout and design of library furniture	
Considerations for layout and design of library furniture	Secondary issues
Provide visible staff desks on each floor to guide readers	Library staff should be visible to aid readers
Provide reader tables in areas well served by natural light	Place tables at edge of library or in internal atria spaces
Divide large reader tables into personal study areas	Provide separate power points along length of table
Ensure mix of table sizes and layouts to suit nature of collection	Atlases and newspapers require different table designs
Ensure tables are connected to IT systems	Encourage mixture of media usage at study tables

Study tables

Table layout is an important consideration since the distribution of reader spaces can influence the configuration of columns and interior walls. Libraries with large book collections increasingly store less frequently used material in basement areas or in other locations. Here modern rolling book stacks can be used to save on space and cost. Basement storage is useful because the high loadings can be more readily accommodated than on upper floors and the reader is not kept waiting too long for the material to be accessed. Reader tables, rather than individual study desks, are the norm, and these are usually placed near the perimeter of the library or in special reader rooms. Tables often allow access for computer laptop machines to be used and there may be a desk lamp and small storage area provided per reader space on a shared table of around eight seating positions. Much depends upon the type of library and the proximity to specialist ICT areas.

An area may need to be set aside for the use of special library materials such as large atlases or maps, broadsheet newspapers and archival material. There may be security issues to consider as well as furniture needs such as large tables. Often there is a need for copying facilities, but photocopiers and printers can create noise and environmental problems. Whereas in public libraries there is often a sharing of tables for a variety of purposes, in academic and professional libraries, study areas are often set aside for specific purposes.

Floor coverings

Floor coverings are usually a long-term choice but need to be flexible for different zones. Therefore it is not always a good idea to have areas carpeted in different colours. Specialist children's rugs and furniture provide more flexibility in their areas, avoiding the committing of a particular area to one function for ever. A lot can be done cheaply with shelving, seating and wall decoration to change the focus of a particular area of the library.

Decisions about library stock, facilities and activities all bear on the choice of furnishings and fittings and the layout of the new facility. Much can be done from the earliest planning stages to ensure there are no last-minute surprises for staff or users in the services that are ultimately offered in the new or refurbished building.

Maintenance

There should be careful consideration of maintenance implications of all specifications to help minimize running costs and ensure long-term viability of the library. Specify robust, high-quality materials and products wherever possible and avoid unusual fixtures and fittings that may cause maintenance and replacement difficulties. The cost of cleaning is also a consideration.

Summary

- There are many elements of design quality to consider; these can be grouped under three headings – urban, building and interior design.

- Urban design is about how the building relates to its environment. Site location and environmental issues are important elements of urban design.

- Building design includes fitness for purpose, efficiency, sustainability and aesthetic quality of the building itself.

- Interior design includes ambience, décor, furniture and floor coverings (where zones are delineated), fixtures and fittings.

- Although interior design takes place towards the end of a project, it is important to consider it from the beginning as it may have implications for other design elements.

- When thinking about the different design elements it is also important to think about the need for flexibility, adaptability to meet future needs and longer-term maintenance implications.

Chapter 10

Space planning and access

Space planning involves determining how large spaces within a building (like rooms and designated areas) are arranged and relate to each other within larger areas. This chapter explores the space planning issues to be considered in library designs.

> When good intentions meet bad planning, library users pay the price.
> (Woodward, 2007, 64)

As with other aspects of project management, space planning involves taking decisions within a finite timescale and within the resources available. Space needs should be forecast and meet a future need, based on the library's projected collection and service aims. Space planning is an important part of library design and will contribute to the success of the library in terms of efficiency.

Access should be as clear and straightforward as possible, with a self-evident layout facilitating independent discovery and study for users. They should not have to understand how the library is structured in order to make use of its services.

When designing a new library, the architect is challenged to bring the sometimes conflicting needs of library and non-library functions into a coherent whole. Typical services provided within a public or academic library might include:

- access to and loan of books
- access to journals and newspapers
- use of workstations
- access to the internet
- electronic access to research journals
- guidance to sources of information
- community and visitor support
- café and refreshment area
- group study activity areas or rooms.

The terms 'relationships' and 'adjacencies' are sometimes used to describe how different areas of a building or space relate to each other. The relationships within a particular library are determined by studying the library's philosophy of service, its use of materials and services and its policies and procedures. Appropriate planning of adjacencies will be critical to the functioning of the library, though these may change in time.

Libraries are service organizations and it is important to consider how they will be used by both users and staff. Planning teams need to consider both relationships and the movement of people and materials through the library during the design process. To operate efficiently, the library must be planned so that there is minimum interference with main routes through the building for both users and materials. Architects need to resolve these relationships through design.

A new library at Dongguan in China has been 'designed according to the density of readers', that is, a pyramidal model with the most dense area at the foot and the least at the top, as follows (foot to top): an activities area, an electronic service area, a circulation area, a research and reference area, and an office area (Dongguan Library, undated).

In the academic sector, a recent publication by HEFCE (2006) gives some useful examples of recent imaginative plans across a wide range of higher education institutions in the UK, showing the way environments can be adapted to meet the needs of staff and student users. This is just a booklet, but it is well illustrated, capturing in photographs and diagrams a range of possibilities open to those planning refurbishments or new builds in this sector. As one contributor notes: 'We spend a lot of time trying to change people. The thing to do is to change the environment and people will change themselves' (Les Watson, Pro-Vice-Chancellor, Glasgow Caledonian University (HEFCE, 2006, 24)).

Common adjacencies

In most libraries, the circulation desk or RFID* (self-service) terminals are located close to the main entrance. This enables users to return books and make enquiries on entering the building and check out materials on their way out. An information or reference desk may also be located within view of the main entrance, so that users can ask for directions when they come into the library.

Collections of current magazines and newspapers in public libraries, and tables and study carrels in academic libraries, are frequently located adjacent to windows so that users have a view of the outside while they are reading and studying. The following lines were especially commissioned from Ted Hughes for inclusion in the document launching 'New Library: the People's Network' in 1997:

Even the most misfitting child
Who's chanced upon the library's worth,
Sits with the genius of the Earth
And turns the key to the whole world.
(Ted Hughes, 'Hear it again', July 1997 (LIC, 1997))

Some common adjacencies in a public library relate to children's areas. Young children should not have to walk through adult spaces to enter the children's area, to walk to the circulation desk, or to use common facilities like a café or toilets. If the library's community meeting room is used for children's story times and activities, the meeting room should be adjacent to the children's area. Within a children's space, school-age young people should not have to walk through a pre-school area to reach their own materials and services.

Another issue to consider when planning adjacencies is noise. At one time, libraries were considered to be quiet spaces, with noise confined, for example, to meeting rooms. In the 21st century many library users have new attitudes about what is an acceptable noise level in a library. Extensive use of computers in libraries has resulted in more conversation between staff and users and between users working at a single computer. Therefore consideration should be given to locating noisy library functions near to each other: circulation desks, browsing areas and, possibly, the entrance to the children's area. Computer-free rooms, quiet reading rooms and individual study rooms placed in adult areas, if located away from the noisy functions, offer spaces where users can read and study in a quiet environment.

Adjacency requirements should describe how each space is to relate to the other spaces around it. There are a number of ways that rooms can relate to each other. Some situations may require good visual communication from one room to another. At other times, the rooms may need to be visually or acoustically isolated. One room might require easy access to one of its neighbours and to be completely separated from another. Sometimes rooms must be placed in close proximity to each other; sometimes they must be separated by as much distance as possible.

Adjacency requirements can be expressed in written form or with graphics. Another option is to draw an adjacency matrix for each area and function of the library, e.g. meeting rooms, children's library, administration, stacks and computer area. Adjacency requirements also need to be addressed in terms of temperature-controlled areas for rare materials and security for a range of materials and equipment. The various adjacencies can be grouped as follows:

■ positive adjacency – spaces are directly related
■ neutral adjacency – spaces share no common relationship
■ negative adjacency – spaces should be separated.

Identifying these distinctions will help in the final design and layout of the library space.

An example of a library space adjacency diagram from Seattle Public Library is in Appendix 4. Here the 'required', 'desired' and 'optional' adjacencies are clearly shown.

The huge variety of reader places include single-person to multi-person tables of various shapes, casual seating, study rooms and group study facilities. Some users like 'active' or noisy social learning environments; others prefer a quiet study environment with good acoustic and visual privacy, and this can be achieved to a degree with varieties of layout and furniture design.

Space requirements

In addition to considering how adjacencies are to be managed, it is important to consider how much space is needed and how it will be used within and between each area. Although there are some specific guidelines for academic libraries, there is no standard for public libraries because of the many variables involved: 'The amount of floor space required by a public library depends on such factors as the unique needs of the individual community, the functions of the library, the level of resources available, the size of the collection, the space available and the proximity of other libraries' (IFLA, 2001).

However, in IFLA's recent library building guidelines (Latimer and Niegaard, 2007) Anders Dahlgren devotes a chapter to 'A practical means of estimating library space needs'. Again, here the many variables mean that there are no definitive tables or checklists, but planners would do well to read through it for their particular requirements. A useful point made by Dahlgren is that a new library is often needed because the existing one has run out of space. As a result staff may have discarded stock rather more rigorously than normal, with the result that the recent net rate of growth is artificially low. The gross rate (the rate at which the library would have grown without the extra discarding) should be used to calculate new space requirements (Dahlgren, 2007, 130).

Table 10.1 provides an outline of suggested space requirements where available.

Table 10.1	Library space requirements	
Type of library	**Space allocation**	**Source/comments**
Public libraries	There are no agreed standards but the following guidelines are available: DCMS: 23 m² per 1000 population (net figure)	DCMS, 2001
	Other research suggests most new library buildings are using a figure of 28–32 m² per 1000 population (gross figure)	Roger Tym and Partners, 2005
	For the purposes of the new 'public libraries national tariff', a measurement of 30 m² per 1000 population is used.	Elson, 2007 See Chapter 7 for more information about the national tariff
Primary schools	The area allocated to the library resource centre should total at least 10 m² plus 0.05 m² for every pupil place	DfES, 2004
	CILIP guidelines discuss some of the issues to consider, but do not include any specific standards	CILIP, 2002
Secondary schools	Students Min m² Max m² 800 340 370 900 370 400 1000 400 440 1100 440 475 1200 470 510 1300 500 550 1400 535 580 1500 570 620	Barrett and Douglas 2004 Note: 'min' = schools for students aged 11–16; max = schools that also have students aged 17–18
	The area allocated to the library resource centre should total at least 50 m² plus 0.1 m² for every pupil place	DfES, 2004
Colleges	Floor space: 1 m² per 10 students Study space: 1 m² per 90 students The total area for further education college learning resource centres should be at least 10% of total college area or a minimum of 20% of the total teaching space	Eynon, 2005 Further information re. number of seats, ICT workspaces, etc. also available (Eynon, 2005)
	2.5 m² per student workspace in resource-based learning rooms or learning resource centres	Eynon, 2005
	Between 2.5 m² and 4 m² per student workspace in higher education	

(continued on next page)

Table 10.1	Continued	
Type of library	Space allocation	Source/comments
Universities	Preferred space standards from the Follett Report are • one space for six full time equivalent students • 2.39 m² per reader • reader modules to be minimum of 900 x 600 mm • information technology space should be 1200 x 800 mm	Follett Report (HEFCE, 1993)
Prison libraries	Minimum size of 93 m² with 'an open space capable of flexibility to reflect changing provision'. Learning space in addition for a minimum of ten offenders with an area of 18.5 m² (1.85 m² per offender)	DfES, 2005, 21

Some sectors differ in their space requirements. For example, in prison libraries, a calm and neutral space is essential. In the past some have used converted cells, which are totally inadequate as library space. Security will be a key concern in this environment, but experience shows that where prisoners are encouraged to feel a sense of ownership of the library through being made welcome, these risks are minimized.

A number of websites offer help with assessing the space requirements of libraries in different sectors (see Bibliography).

Population and use data

An important part of the space-planning process is to research population figures. This will include, in the case of public libraries, the resident population and the number of people coming to work in the catchment area. Academic libraries will have finite numbers of students, but the needs of these students will vary depending on the course they are studying, their learning style and the type of student that they are (e.g. part-time, full-time, mature). There may also be a policy of opening up particular collections and facilities to members of the general public doing their own research.

Data about these things will need to be collected for planning purposes. Using this information, librarians and trustees should be able to estimate their library's space needs in terms of square footage and to determine if a more detailed study is required. In preparation for this it would be appropriate to classify the existing service point according to the broad types of space discussed below, which relate to arrangement by function. The librarian should also identify collections or service areas that are not being considered in the project.

The architect will need further information from the librarian in order to progress the project. This will include the number of users in the library daily. Figures should ideally relate to particular areas of the library and take into account the projected usage of the new facility and not necessarily what is currently catered for. In order to determine space needs it will be necessary to observe library users, evaluate existing facilities and compare with other communities. It will also be important to consider:

- opening hours (all or part of the library, including out-of-hours)
- peak usage times
- usage broken down by hours
- days of the week library open
- times of the year (particularly for university/college libraries)
- number of users (preferably separate figures for each part of the library)
- associated activities, e.g. meeting rooms, exhibition area(s)
- facilities, e.g. toilets, vending area, café
- staff services to users – how many staff will be on duty/service points, security points
- staff facilities, e.g. workroom, offices, post room, services, storage.

The primary roles and mission of the library will affect the size of the different collections. For example, if the main role of the public library is to be a popular library, then the library features current, high-demand, high-interest materials in a variety of formats for users of all ages. Such a facility would promote browsing and have attractive displays and good signage with casual seating. However, if the main role is to encourage children in their early years, then the library would focus on services for children and for parents and children together. The facility would need to be in a location easily accessible to young children, with sufficient inviting space for activities and story times. Conversely, a research library would have very different requirements.

The architect will require details of specific areas of the library and then work with the librarian to complete a functional area sheet, a room schedule or a room data sheet for each area of the library. Figure 10.1 gives an example of such a form.

Name of area: Circulation desk   **Dimensions**: 200 sq. ft.

Activities: Staff operate a desk for the checkout and return of library material up to 600 items a day. Also need to register new users and deal with routine customer enquiries in person and by telephone.

Major design features and ambience of area: This area must be capable of handling a significant number of customers. It should be inviting and have efficient flow for users. The layout should allow space for limited queuing.

Furniture and equipment: A counter 10 x 5 ft. with modular units, with ease of exit for library staff. Drawers for materials and stationery. House 3 trolleys. Storage of 600 books/DVDs.

Seating: 4 seats for staff working on PCs and 2 stools. 2 chairs for customers.

Materials: facilities to return material – including approx. 300 books per day.
Occupancy: Public: 7–10   Staff: 4   Daily use: 2000

Relationship and connections: Near entrance/exits of building, visible to public areas and near security office. Located away from quiet areas.

Layout and flexibility: In order to maintain this area's appearance, the space should be designed to make it extremely difficult to have it filled with clutter. RFID to be introduced at a later date and will need to modify this area to accommodate this new technology.

Technical requirements, e.g. environments – lighting, heating and security:
Sound – Given this area's heavy use, it is essential that the design helps to dampen sound. Adequate ventilation and protection from cold draughts are important for staff at this location.

Special requirements: Require 4 PCs. The level of the desk should be appropriate to disabled users. The design should incorporate fixed holders for leaflets and a plasma screen mounted on the wall.

Information provided by: the person who was interviewed for this particular functional area.

Date: the last date this sheet was written or modified.

Figure 10.1 Example of a room schedule/functional area sheet (adapted from Lushington, 2002, 50)

Types of space

In the context of the whole space required, the various web resources agree
on the following seven types of space to be considered in a new library
building:

- collection space
- electronic workstation space
- user seating space
- staff work space
- meeting space
- special use space
- non-assignable space (including mechanical space for heating and other
  systems).

Each of these is dealt with in more detail below.

Collection space

A room without books is like a body without a soul.

(Marcus Tullius Cicero, Roman politician)

Collection space needs to take account of books (open access and closed),
periodicals (display and back issues) and non-print resources. Digital
resources may need some space allocation. The Whole Building Design
Guide (WBDG; www.wbdg.org) has a section on its website for different
types of building. Within the pages about public libraries there are
detailed descriptions of ways to calculate floor space needed for a particular
type of material, taking into account the expected life of the building. The
guide notes that: 'The number of volumes of books, non-print materials
. . . and periodicals . . . can change from 5 to 25 volumes per square foot
depending on shelf height, aisle width and the kind of material, whether
it's magazines or encyclopaedias.'

The pages of the website note with books, for example, that a rule of
thumb is to estimate the total number of volumes needed, say, over 20 years
and to divide this number by 10. For compact storage, the division should
be by 25. Thus if the collection over 20 years is deemed to be 50,000

volumes, when divided by 10 this gives 5000 which is the number of square feet of space required (see www.wbdg.org./design/public_library).

The calculation for periodicals is more complicated, depending on whether space is required for back issues.

Electronic workstation space

Electronic workstation space needs to be calculated for staff use, public use in the main area as well as any need in meeting room areas. A public access catalogue used from a seated position requires 40 ft^2; that used standing requires 20 ft^2. If the workstation is to allow for users to bring their own equipment, 75 ft^2 may be needed. For microfiche and microfilm readers 35 ft^2 is deemed appropriate.

User seating space

User seating space must take account of seats needed at tables or alone. WBDG recommends for public areas (not staff areas or meeting rooms) that there are 5 seats per 1000 users. Table seating requires 25 ft^2, a study carrel 30 ft^2 and lounge chairs 35 ft^2. A useful average is 30 ft^2 per chair.

Staff work space

Staff work space can include areas in the public part of the library as well as separate work room facilities. WBDG recommends 150 ft^2 per work area (e.g. issue counter, help desk). The guide states: 'As a general rule of thumb, the square footage allotment for staff work areas equals the number of projected staff areas multiplied by 150.'

Meeting space

Areas for meetings may include conference space, a lecture theatre or a room for children's activities. When calculating seat space, the square footage for lecture-style chairs would be the total number of chairs multiplied by 10. For conference-style seating the figure would be multiplied by 25. Seating for children's activities would require 10 square feet per seat. Space would also need to be allocated to other functions like kitchen facilities or storage space for equipment.

Special use space

Special use space will be peculiar to the project's particular needs. The library might require a local history room, a job centre, tourist information centre or it might house a special collection of some kind with appropriate facilities for users to access the material. WBDG offers a table of square footage measurements required for particular items like map files, microfilm cabinets and display cases. Generally, suppliers of equipment should include this detail in their catalogues.

Non-assignable space

Non-assignable space may be important to the running of the library but is not related to services offered directly by the library. It may include toilets, stairs, lifts, corridors and space required for heating or other systems on which the library depends. In general, non-assignable space accounts for between 20% and 30% of the gross floor area of a library.

Storage

The more activities a building accommodates the more storage it needs, especially where rooms are used for different functions (e.g. children's workshops, community meetings).

Design for accessibility

It is widely recognized that those who use libraries have a wide range of capabilities and that the needs of those who have specific physical or sensory impairments often coincide with the needs of many other users. The design solution to this is the integrated, all inclusive approach. The library environmental design should be broad enough overall and in detail to suit the widest practicable range of customers, including people with disabilities.

There are therefore many issues around access to library services which the manager of a new library project should address. The disability logo of a figure in a wheelchair perpetuates the idea in many managers' minds that disabled access is for those in wheelchairs only. The astute manager will examine access issues across the range of potential impairments, including the needs of the hearing-impaired, visually impaired and those with mobility difficulties who are not in wheelchairs, as well as those with impaired fine motor skills. Access is required both to the physical building and to the collections, including computer resources. Central to access issues is the Disability Discrimination Act 1995.

The Disability Discrimination Act 1995*

This act requires the removal of all physical barriers to the accessing of services, in order to ensure that they are available to those with sight, hearing, mobility or learning disabilities. New buildings need to be 'DDA-compliant' and older buildings altered. In the case of older buildings obstacles can be insurmountable, particularly in the case of listed buildings. As regards library buildings and equipment, particular attention will need to be paid to accessibility and the provision of assistive technology, including regard to the needs of wheelchair users.

The physical environment

The aim is to ensure that disabled people can approach, enter, navigate and use public library spaces as easily as non-disabled people. Subjects for consideration include accessing the library, décor and signs, and facilities.

Accessing the library

Consider:

- parking – including parking bays for people with disabilities within easy reach of the library
- approach to building (e.g. dropped curbs, signage)
- entrance accessibility (e.g. ramps, steps and handrails)
- doors (exterior and interior); dignified access for all; accessible route(s)
- lifts and stair lifts
- access for people with physical disabilities to all parts of the library including shelving, services and facilities
- keeping aisles, corridors, doorways and spaces free of obstruction and sufficiently spacious to accommodate wheelchair users

- means for people with disabilities to leave the building quickly in the event of an emergency
- alarm systems suitable for alerting deaf people
- critical distances (for example, width of corridors and aisles, width of security sensors)
- library layout such as to aid orientation and navigation.

Décor and signs

Consider:

- floor surfaces and coverings – colour contrasts
- windows – low enough for wheelchair users to see out
- lighting – task lighting to assist the disabled
- good colour contrasts in decoration schemes
- finishes and furnishings that inhibit dust retention
- slip-resistant floor finishes
- switches and controls
- signs (for example, Braille signs and shelf marks)
- buzzer for alert/attention or to gain assistance
- notices concerning available services and opening times
- signage – size and finish
- signage – incorporation of symbols as well as words.

Facilities

Consider:

- toilets – for the disabled including wheelchair access
- loop systems at counters and enquiry desks
- textphone facilities
- stability of furniture and fittings
- furniture and fittings placed so as not to obstruct circulation
- equipment intended for public use (e.g. photocopiers) at accessible locations and heights
- seating with good back and arm support
- desks and study spaces suitable for wheelchair users

- furniture and equipment height (for example, shelving, tables, counters and photocopiers accessible by users seated in wheeled vehicles)
- meeting rooms
- emergency facilities – alarms, visual as well as audible.

Consideration must also be given to information access, e.g. assistive technology such as speech OPACs.

Impact

The impact of access needs on different types of library renewal is illustrated in Figure 10.2. For example, a brand new library should enable maximum accessibility, but this might come at a higher cost.

Library improvement	Time	Cost	Impact
New library building	High	High	High
Extension to existing building			
Major refurbishment			
New furniture and equipment	⬆	⬆	⬆
Reordering of existing library			
Internal reorganization	Low	Low	Low

Figure 10.2   Impact of access needs on library builds

Kits of parts

Working with the architect and internal design consultants, the librarian will need to establish the types of seating and shelving required in the new library, the appropriate sizes for these elements and the amount of space that would be required between the elements. There follow examples or 'kits of parts', which might be useful to consider for the proposed library project. These suggested heights and measures will vary depending on the type of library or the configuration of the layout and if the shelves are, for example, open or closed access. Functional requirements for the following elements may vary:

- reference library
- lending library
- archives and local studies
- children's library
- music or multimedia library
- open and closed access shelving
- staff areas.

The new metric handbook for architects, which contains planning and design data on the main building types from airports to auditoria, has a section for libraries which contains measurement and height details. However, this text does not distinguish between various types of libraries. The *Metric Handbook* (Littlefield, 2008) is published by the Architectural Press. The other key text that architects may also refer to is the international handbook of architects' data (Neufert et al., 2000).

Kits of parts follow for these features: shelf stacks; shelving plan options; shelving; tables; DDA-compliant counters; wheelchair access; wheelchair reach.

Shelf stacks

Consider access issue as well as functional requirements, e.g. books above/below average eye level or reach (as in Figure 10.3 below).

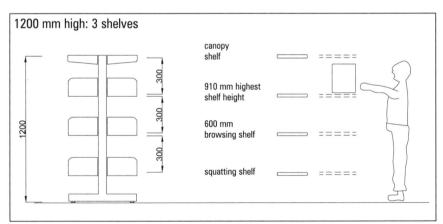

Figure 10.3 Requirements of shelf stacks

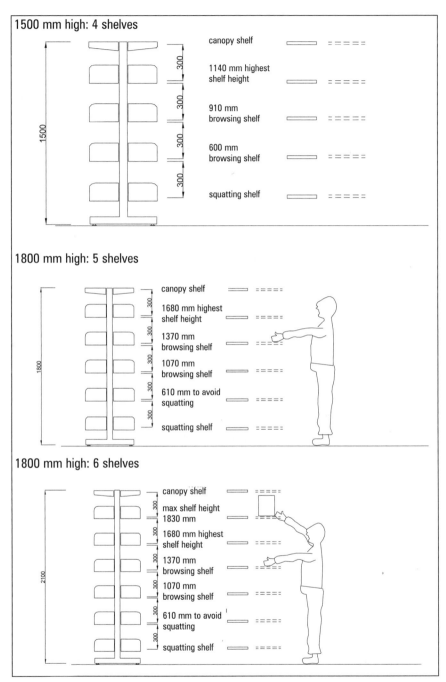

Figure 10.3 *Continued*

Shelving plan options

Note – DDA-compliant layout requires wheelchair access between shelves.

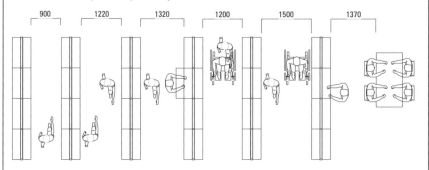

Shelving

Considerations might be:
to accommodate single file (walking) – 500 mm between
to accommodate double file – 1220 mm between.

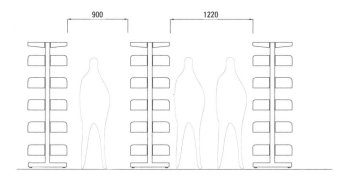

Tables

Layout suggestions to accommodate different needs, e.g. formal/informal and movement between them.

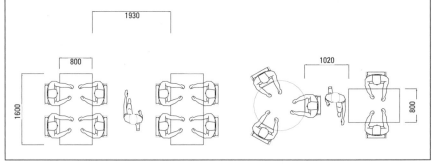

Figure 10.3 *Continued*

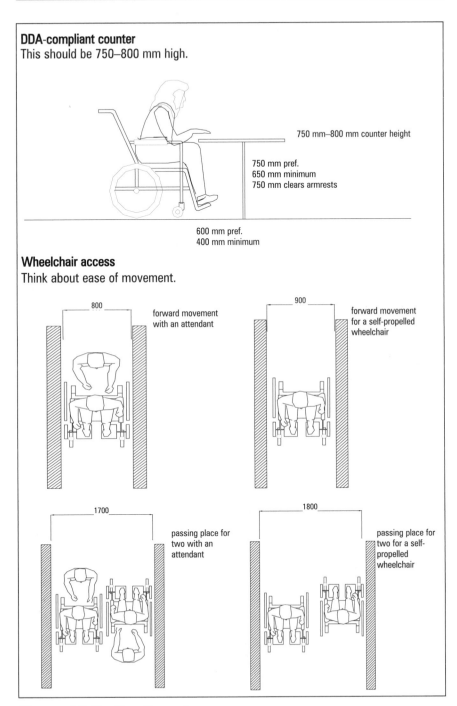

DDA-compliant counter
This should be 750–800 mm high.

750 mm–800 mm counter height

750 mm pref.
650 mm minimum
750 mm clears armrests

600 mm pref.
400 mm minimum

Wheelchair access
Think about ease of movement.

800
forward movement
with an attendant

900
forward movement
for a self-propelled
wheelchair

1700
passing place for
two with an
attendant

1800
passing place for
two for a self-
propelled
wheelchair

Figure 10.3 *Continued*

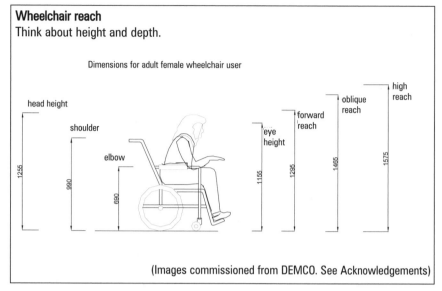

Wheelchair reach
Think about height and depth.

Dimensions for adult female wheelchair user

(Images commissioned from DEMCO. See Acknowledgements)

Figure 10.3 *Continued*

Summary

- Space planning is the process of determining how spaces are used inside the building.
- 'Relationships and adjacencies' describe how spaces are organized – which areas can be next to each other, or not, as appropriate.
- In addition to thinking about adjacencies, consideration must be given to the types and amounts of space required; data from various sources will be used to determine these things, e.g. population data, levels of use of different parts of the service.
- The Disability Discrimination Act sets standards in relation to accessibility, for example space, lighting and signage.
- The type of furniture used, e.g. heights of shelves, can have a huge impact on the experience of library users and staff.

Chapter 11

Occupancy and post-occupancy evaluation

> Building occupancy is an area of planning that is often forgotten. Once the building phase is over, there is other work to be done. There needs to be careful preparation and planning for 'the move'. There also needs to be an evaluation process. This chapter briefly explores these.

> Undoubtedly there is still a role for the information professional in a physical space. The adaptability of that space will be increasingly important.   (Angela Dove (Dove, 2004, 24))

The first year in a new building can be almost as stressful as the time leading up to the move. No new building is free from flaws, and there will be a number of construction mistakes to deal with. Also, only when the building is functioning will staff find out how people really use it, and the best laid plans can be thwarted by the flow of the new building dynamics. So this must be built into the planning and budget process.

Handover

This is a formal procedure in which the building is explained to the client who then takes on full ownership and responsibility for its management.

Moving in

The move itself needs to be planned – possibly phased – and staff need to be given an opportunity to familiarize themselves with the building and the equipment.

The first few months in a new building are by far the most testing. All kinds of unexpected problems can occur. This is normal and the librarian and others involved should not be too hard on themselves.

Even if construction has been uneventful and the building is on schedule, it might be advisable to delay moving in valuable material or archival collections, so the environment can settle.

When the building is handed over to the client, many systems need to be tested in normal use, such as lifts, lights, security systems, heating, plumbing and drainage. As equipment starts to be used, the system needs balancing until everything works as planned. This is quite usual in the early days. Although many systems will need to be tested and fine-tuned, some, like heating and ventilation systems, may need a full cycle of use over a whole year in order to be fully tested.

The following issues need to be addressed and budgeted for if the manager decides to go ahead with them:

- establishment of a 'move committee' to plan the actual move and any preparatory work to collections
- measurement of stock to be moved to ensure it will fit into the new space (this should have been done in the project brief)
- appointment of a specialist firm to undertake the move
- schedule for all procedures
- closure of existing library
- transfer of existing furniture, collections or shelves to the new site
- repair or cleaning of stock or equipment before the move
- cataloguing of any parts of collection
- induction sessions for staff
- opening of the new library including phased opening

- the official opening (preferably at least three months after opening to allow time for the building to settle down and any minor changes in the operation of the building to take place)
- marketing to be in place for promoting the new building and its services.

Evaluation

When the project is finished, there are two types of evaluation that need to be undertaken in order to learn effectively from the experience. The first relates to the project processes, the second to the reaction of users and staff to the new facilities.

Evaluation of the process

Monitoring against the original objectives is an important part of checking that the business case for the new or refurbished library has been met. The types of question to ask include:

- Was the building completed on time and within budget?
- Were substantial changes made to the original design?
- Were there any maintenance difficulties?
- Did the architect provide all the services specified in the contract?
- How was the working relationship between the project team and architect?
- Were all the objectives in the original design brief met?
- Were there any other learning points for future projects?

Reaction to the library building

It is difficult to anticipate the reaction of users and staff. It is therefore wise to allow time and resources for post-occupancy building work and minor changes to the library to be implemented as a result of actual use. The changes that are made are likely to result from feedback from stakeholders, obtained through an evaluation process. Depending on the size of the new building, it might be a good idea to set up a co-ordinating group which meets regularly to talk through any problems – there are examples of this having worked well.

There are two basic types of evaluation: quantitative and qualitative:

Quantitative evaluation concerns numbers – items that can be counted. The kind of quantitative information that might prove useful relates to service use, for example:

■ comparison of usage with what was anticipated; it is important here to consider not just numbers but also user profiles, especially if the project aimed to target specific groups
■ frequency of visits by individual users
■ extent to which particular areas or facilities are being used and by whom.

This type of data can provide hard evidence about the impact of the project.

Qualitative evaluation examines data that cannot be counted, for example, experiences, feelings and expectations. Surveys of staff and users, in the short and longer term, could ask about:

■ opinions of the new building
■ feelings of users when they are in the building
■ favourite parts of the building
■ comparison with their expectations.

Evaluation could be conducted in conjunction with groups involved in the community engagement process. Alternatively, evaluation could be undertaken by a member of library staff or contracted to an independent consultant. The approach taken will depend partly on previous consultation and partly on the resources available.

In addition to providing evidence that may be of use to this project, evaluation data can support the development of future projects by providing evidence of effectiveness. However, if no evaluation is undertaken, a valuable opportunity to learn and continue to improve current and future services will be lost.

Monitoring energy consumption

In the present climate (natural and political) targets need to be established for environmental standards and energy consumption. These then need to be monitored over a period – discrepancies may relate to specific climate conditions or may be caused by the control systems not operating effectively or staff not following agreed procedures.

The greatest costs of the library building are incurred after it is built, on maintenance, repairs, day-to-day management, cleaning, security etc. A library is relatively inexpensive to build in relation to the overall running costs during its life and the investment in people while it is in use. The planning and design decisions made much earlier in the project have a major influence on these subsequent maintenance costs. It is important that the staff who will be responsible for running costs and specialists such as the facilities manager are engaged in the project at an early stage.

Summary

- It is important to remember that the project does not end when the new building opens. There are bound to be some flaws and issues to be resolved and the plan needs to accommodate them.
- It is also important to evaluate the project at two levels: the process itself – the project management and design – and the experience and perceptions of staff and users in relation to the new building.
- Evaluation of the new building may be useful in the short and longer term, to support the current project and to provide evidence to support the development of future projects.

Chapter 12

Building libraries for the future – a summary

The physical library is undergoing a major transformation from collection-centric to user-focused space, in line with changes in society and a rapid pace of technological development. Within the broader framework of a knowledge society, libraries are shifting in focus from collections to connections and away from an emphasis on storage and access, although the priority given to each will depend on the mission, culture and aims of the library service.

Any new library should recognize the importance of people, books, ICT and the complex and dynamic relationships between them. Skilful architects and expert planners will strike a clearer balance between creating functional and inspiring buildings with exciting architectural features and enjoyable internal spaces.

Any library or information professional practitioner who is in the position of managing the refurbishment or new building of a library should grasp this challenge for the opportunities it offers to see through an exciting new development for the parent institution, be it a school, university or community facility.

The building programme must encompass a business case, clear parameters for the management of the project, close working from the outset with a design team, whose members, particularly the architect, share the vision for the project, and a robust design brief. Engagement with the whole community from the pre-planning stage through to the opening of the new building and beyond will ensure a sense of ownership in that community and added value to the services offered as well as appropriate take-up of the new facilities.

The members of the project management team will have to negotiate unforeseen changes, however careful and considered their planning, and this will necessitate a flexible, open approach to the exterior and interior design of the building. Even after opening, the team will need to make changes as staff and users adapt to their new surroundings.

The future of the library as a physical 'place' has been a matter of considerable debate in recent years. Despite some hasty predictions about the death of libraries and growth of virtual worlds, libraries continue to be created around the world, often, as it happens, with growing printed collections as well as exhibition and meeting spaces. Rather than being replaced by ICT, libraries have welcomed the technology, which has contributed to their becoming vibrant and relevant centres of culture, learning and community. Many new and refurbished buildings reflect this developed role, encouraging libraries to remain relevant in the 21st century and beyond. Higher standards of education and the 'information explosion' have contributed to the rise in the number of new library buildings as well as the expansion and re-modelling of existing provision.

The key challenge for the managers and design team in a library project is understanding how people interact with, and are influenced by, the environment that surrounds them. A library can be one of the most important buildings within a community and should express the values of that community. Civic buildings reflect and contribute to local culture and heritage, sometimes having even wider national or international cultural status. It is therefore crucial that any library design team should appreciate the importance of the task being undertaken, not least because of the numbers of people who will be affected by the finished project. Therefore a well designed library should be welcoming and accessible, encouraging existing and new users to cross the threshold and engage with activities taking place inside. All libraries should make a positive contribution to the public realm and be fit for purpose. The public space should be easily navigable, allowing users to find their way with a minimum of signs. It is hoped that this book has cleared a path through the design and building process for 21st-century libraries that is equally navigable.

Bibliography and further reading

This is in two parts – texts and websites. Most texts have been referred to in the body of the book, but some are added in for further reading. Websites are listed alphabetically by the organization.

Texts

Adler, D. (1999) *Metric Handbook: planning and design data*, Architectural Press.

Barber, P. and Wallace, L. (2007) Our Kind of Town: how the Chicago public library is changing the city, *American Libraries*, April (Design issue), 56–62.

Barlow, A. and Morris, A. (2007) *Usability of Public Libraries: perceptions and experiences of new users, World Library and Information Congress, 73rd IFLA General Conference and Council*, 19-23 August 2007, Durban, South Africa, www.ifla.org/iv/ifla73/index.htm.

Barrett, L. and Douglas, J. (2004) *CILIP Guidelines for Secondary School Libraries*, Facet Publishing (chapter devoted to facilities management, which includes a section on space requirements).

Birmingham City Council (2001) *Prospectus for the New Library of Birmingham*, www.birmingham.gov.uk/libraries.

Bisbrouck, M.-F. and Chauveinc, M. (eds) (1999) *Intelligent Library*

Buildings: proceedings of the tenth seminar of the IFLA Section on Library Buildings and Equipment, The Hague, 24–29 August 1997, K. G. Saur.

Browne, M. (ed.) (1981) *Joint Use Libraries in the Australian community: proceedings of a national workshop,* Melbourne, 13–15 August 1980, National Library of Australia.

Bryson, J., Usherwood, R. and Proctor, R. (2003) *Libraries Must Also Be Buildings? New library impact study,* Department of Information Studies, University of Sheffield, http://cplis.shef.ac.uk/New%20Library%20Impact%20Study.pdf.

BS 5454 (1989) *Recommendations for Storage and Exhibition of Archival Documents,* British Standards Institution.

Bundy, A. (1983) *Widening Client Horizons: joint use public libraries, progress and potential,* www.library.unisa.edu.au/about/papers/widen.pdf.

Bury Metro Libraries (2006) Outreach Library Service Position Paper, January 2006, www.mlanorthwest.org.uk/assets/documents/1000027Foutreach LibraryServicePositionPaper-January2006.pdf.

CABE (2003) *Creating Excellent Buildings: a guide for clients,* www.cabe.org.uk/AssetLibrary/4037.pdf.

CABE (2006a) *Better Public Building,* produced on behalf of HM Government by CABE and DCMS, http://cabe.org.uk/AssetLibrary/9282.pdf.

CABE (2006b) *Design Review: how CABE evaluates quality in architecture and urban design,* www.cabe.org.uk/AssetLibrary/8642.pdf.

CABE and Resource (2003) *Better Public Libraries,* www.cabe.org.uk/AssetLibrary/2151.pdf.

Cannon, J. A (2005) *Making the Business Case: how to create, write and implement a successful business plan,* Chartered Institute of Personnel and Development.

Charlton, L. (1992) *Designing and Planning a Secondary School Library Resource Centre,* School Library Association.

CILIP (2002) *The Primary School Library: guidelines*, rev. edn, www.cilip.org.uk/professionalguidance/sectors/youngpeople/ primaryguidelines.htm.

CILIP (2007) *Designed for Learning: school libraries*, CILIP School Libraries Group, Production Company Yorkshire Ltd, DVD.

Collis, R. and Boden, L. (1997) *Guidelines for Prison Libraries*, 2nd edn, Library Association Publishing.

Commonwealth Schools Commission (1983) *School/community Libraries in Australia: report to the Commonwealth Schools Commission.*

Connecticut State Library (2002) *Library Space Planning Guide*, www.cslib.org/libbuild.htm.

Dahlgren, A. (1996) *Planning the Small Library Facility*, 2nd edn, Small Libraries Publication 23, Library Administration and Management Association.

Dahlgren, A. (2007) A Practical Means of Estimating Library Space Needs. In Latimer, K. and Niegaard, H. (2007) *IFLA Library Buildings Guidelines: development and reflections*, K. G. Saur, 127–43.

Dahlgren, A. (1998) *Public Library Space Needs: a planning guide*, State of Wisconsin, Department of Public Instruction – Public Library Development, http://dpi.wi.gov/pld/plspace.html.

DCMS (2003) *Framework for the Future*, Department of Culture, Media and Sport, www.culture.gov.uk/Reference_library/Publications/archive_ 2003/framework_future.htm.

DCMS (2004) *Culture at the Heart of Regeneration*, PP631, www.culture.gov.uk/images/consultations/DCMSCulture.pdf.

Dewe, M. (2006) *Planning Public Library Buildings: concepts and issues for the librarian*, Ashgate.

DfES (2004a) *Area Guidelines for Schools*, www.teachernet.gov.uk/management/resourcesfinanceandbuilding/ schoolbuildings/designguidance/sbareaguidelines/.

DfES (2004b) *Briefing Framework for Primary School Projects*, Building Bulletin 99, www.teachernet.gov.uk.

DfES (2004c) *Briefing Framework for Secondary School Projects*, Building Bulletin 98, www.teachernet.gov.uk.

DfES (2005) *The Offender, Library, Learning and Information Specification (OLLIS)*, Department for Education and Science with Home Office, Offenders' Learning and Skills Unit, www.cilip.org.uk/specialinterestgroups/bysubject/prison/publications/ollis.htm.

Dolan, J. and Khan, A. (2002) The Library of Birmingham, *Library and Information Update*, **1** (4), April, 34–6.

Dongguan Library (undated) Dongguan Library: a metro-center library striding into the 21st century, (leaflet promoting the new Dongguan central library in China, opened in 2005).

Dove, A. (2004) Designing Space for Knowledge Work, *Library and Information Update*, **3** (3), March, 22–4.

Edwards, B. and Fisher, B. (2002) *Libraries and Learning Resource Centres*, Architectural Press.

Edwards, B. with Khan, A. (2008) Libraries and Information Centres. In Littlefield, D. (ed.), *Metric Handbook*, Architectural Press, Chapter 29.

Eley, J. (2003) Creating Excellent Buildings: a guide for clients, CABE, www.cabe.org.uk/default.aspx?contentitemid=450.

Elson, M. (2007) *The National Public Library Tariff*, The Museums, Libraries and Archives Council.

Enright, S. (2002) Post-occupancy Evaluation of UK Library Building Projects: some examples of current activity, offprint from *Liber Quarterly*, **12**, 26–45.

Eynon, A. (ed.) (2005) *Guidelines for Colleges: recommendations for learning resources*, Colleges of Further and Higher Education Group of CILIP, Facet Publishing.

Faulkner-Brown, H. (1999): Some Thoughts on the Design of Major Library Buildings. In Bisbrouck, M. and Chauveinc, M. (eds). *Intelligent Library Buildings: proceedings of the tenth seminar of the IFLA Section on Library Buildings and Equipment*, The Hague, 24–29 August 1997, K. G. Saur.

Finch, P. (2000) *Better Public Buildings: a proud legacy for the future*,

Department of Culture, Media and Sport,
www.culture.gov.uk/NR/rdonlyres/31A1350C-E0A4-4118-8856-A015E34D6E64/0/better_pub_buildings1.pdf.

Fine, J. W. (2001) *Building Blocks for Planning Functional Library Space*, Library Administration and Management Association, Scarecrow Press.

Harper, P. (2006) Library Design has Arrived, *Library and Information Update*, **5** (7-8), 35-9 (part of a special issue on library design).

Harriman, J. H. P. (2008) *Creating Your Library's Business Plan: a how-to-do-it manual with samples on CD-ROM*, Neal-Schuman Inc. and Facet Publishing.

Harris, G. and Marshall, J. G. (1996) Building a Model Business Case: current awareness service in a special library, *Special Libraries*, Summer, 181-94.

Harrison, D. (ed.) (1995) *Library Buildings 1990–1994*, Library Association Publishing.

Haviland, D. (2001) *You and Your Architect*, American Institute of Architects,
www.aia.org/SiteObjects/files/youandyourarchitect.pdf.

Hawthorne, P. and Martin, R. G. (eds) (1995) *Planning Additions to Academic Library Buildings*, American Library Association.

HEFCE (1999) *Joint Funding Council's Libraries Review Group: Report* (The Follett Report),
www.ujoln.ac.uk/services/papers/follett/report.

HEFCE (2006) *Designing Spaces for Effective Learning: a guide to twenty-first century learning space design*, JISC e-learning programme, www.jisc.ac.uk.

Huffine, R. (2004) *Business Case for Information Services: EPA's regional libraries and centers*, US Environmental Protection Agency, www.epa.gov/natlibra/epa260r04001.pdf.

IFLA (2001) *The Public Library Service: IFLA/UNESCO guidelines for development*, prepared by a working group chaired by Philip Gill on behalf of the Section of Public Libraries, K. G. Saur, IFLA Publications 97, www.ifla.org/VII/s8/proj/publ97.pdf.

JISC (2006) *Designing Spaces for Effective Learning: a guide to 21st century learning space design,* Joint Information Systems Committee, www.jisc.ac.uk/eli_learningspaces.html.

Kugler, C. (2007) Interior Design Considerations and Developing the Brief. In Latimer, K. and Niegaard, H. (2007) *IFLA Library Buildings Guidelines: development and reflections,* K. G. Saur, 144–71.

Latimer, K. and Niegaard, H. (eds) (2007) *IFLA Library Building Guidelines: developments and reflections,* K. G. Saur.

Library Association Information Services Group (1999) *Guidelines for Reference and Information Services in Public Libraries,* Library Association Publishing. (Has some advice on the principles behind the identification and use of space within a library is given in chapter 5).

LIC (1997) *New Library: the People's Network,* Library and Information Commission, www.ukoln.ac.uk/services/lisc/newlibrary/contents.html.

Littlefield, D. (2008) *Metric Handbook: planning and design data,* 3rd edn, Architectural Press.

Lushington, N. (2002) *Libraries Designed for Users: a 21st century guide,* Neal-Schuman.

Lushington, N. (2008) *Libraries Designed for Kids,* Neal Schuman Inc. and Facet Publishing.

McCabe, G. B. (2000) *Planning for a New Generation of Public Library Buildings,* Greenwood Press.

McCarthy, R. C. (2000) *Designing Better Libraries: selecting and working with building professionals,* Handbook Series, Highsmith Press.

McDermott, N. (2007) Inspiring Public Spaces: the 2007 Public Library Buildings Awards UK & Republic of Ireland, PowerPoint presentation to Public Library Authorities' Conference, 10 October 2007.

McDonald, A. (2007) *The Top Ten Qualities of Good Library Space.* In Latimer, K. and Niegaard, H. *IFLA Library Buildings Guidelines: development and reflections,* K. G. Saur, 13–29.

McNicol, S. (2008) *Joint-use Libraries: libraries for the future,* Information Series, Chandos Press.

MLA (2008) *Public Libraries, Archives and New Development: a standard charge approach*, The Museums, Libraries and Archives Council, www.mla.gov.uk/resources/assets//P/Public_Libraries__Archives _and_New_Development_A_standard_charge_approach_13345. pdf.

MLA/CSV Consulting (2006) *Community Engagement in Public Libraries: a report on current practice and future developments*, www.mla.gov.uk/resources/assets//C/community_engagement_ report_9654.pdf.

NAO (2004) *Getting Citizens Involved: community participation in neighbourhood renewal*, National Audit Office, Report by the Comptroller and Auditor General, www.nao.org.uk/publications/nao_reports/03-04/03041070.pdf.

Neufert, E. et al. (2000) *Neufert Architects' Data*, 3rd edn, Blackwell.

Noruzi, A. (2004) *Application of Ranganathan's Laws to the Web*, www.webology.ir/2004/v1n2/a8.html.

OCLC (2003) *2003 Environment Scan: executive summary*, www.oclc.org/info/escan/c.

ODPM (2005a) *Your Neighbourhood: getting involved and having a say*, an introduction to the discussion document 'Citizen Engagement and Public Services: why neighbourhoods matter', www.communities.gov.uk/documents/localgovernment/pdf/ 143429.pdf.

ODPM and Home Office (2005) *Citizen Engagement and Public Services: why neighbourhoods matter*, Office of the Deputy Prime Minister and Home Office, www.communities.gov.uk/documents/localgovernment/pdf/ 143234.

O'Reilly, J. J. N. (1987) *Better Briefing Means Better Buildings*, BRE Press.

Phillips, R. (2000) *Architect's Plan of Work*, Royal Institute of British Architects. Update of the definitive RIBA *Outline Plan of Work*, 1998, with its definition of key stages A–L.

Pickard, Q. (2002) *The Architect's Handbook*, Royal Institute of British Architects.

Ranganathan, S. R. (1931) *Five Laws of Library Science*, Madras Library Association, http://dlist.sir.arizona.edu/1220/.

Resource (2003) *Security in Museums, Archives and Libraries: a practical guide*, www.mla.gov.uk/resources/assets//S/security_manual_pdf_5900.pdf.

RIBA (1999) *Engaging an Architect: guidance for clients to quality based selection*, Royal Institute of British Architects.

Robinson, L. (2005) *Writing a Business Case to Improve Organisational Impact*, presentation to the Special Libraries Association Conference, Toronto, Canada, June 2005, www.lesleyrobinson.co.uk/presentations/Making_a_business_case_article.pdf.

Roger Tym and Partners (2005) *The Costs and Funding of Growth in South East England*, www.mlasoutheast.org.uk/aboutus/publications/reports/index.asp?id=1691,1247,7,1251.

Sannwald, W. W. (2001) *Checklist of Library Building Design Considerations*, 4th edn, American Library Association.

Schilpf, F. and Moorman, J. (1998) *The Seven Deadly Sins of Public Library Architecture* (5pp – updated 31 March 2006 to explain the 'sins' in more detail), www.urbanafreelibrary.org/departments/presentations/fredarch.pdf.

Schmidt, J. (2007) Unlocking the library: library design from a marketing perspective. In Latimer, K. and Niegaard, H., *IFLA Library Buildings Guidelines: development and reflections*, K. G. Saur, 55-67.

Taney, K. B. (2003) *Teen Spaces: the step-by-step library makeover*, American Library Association.

Thompson, G. (1989) *Planning and Design of Library Buildings*, 3rd edn, Architectural Press (also 1st ed of 1973).

Woodward, J. (2000) *Countdown to a New Library: managing the building project*, American Library Association.

Woodward, J. (2007) Human Error, *American Libraries*, April (Design issue), 64-6.

Woodworth, E. (2002) *BC Ministry of Health Library business case: does the Minister of Health Planning/Services need a library service? A zero-base business approach*, http://hlabc.bc.ca/fileadmin/ fe-downloads/MOH_Case.pdf.

Worpole, K. (2004) *21st Century Libraries: changing forms, changing futures*, Building Futures, www.buildingfutures.org.uk/pdfs/pdffile_31.pdf.

Websites

American Institute of Architects
www.aia.org

Architecture + Design Scotland
www.ads.org.uk

Better Public Building
The Better Public Building Initiative, established in 2005 in association with CABE. This provides links to design resources and lists the winners and shortlisted buildings for the Prime Minister's Better Public Buildings Award including some libraries.
www.betterpublicbuilding.org.uk

Building Research Establishment Environmental Assessment Method (BREEAM)
www.breeam.org/index.jsp

Chartered Institute of Library and Information Professionals (CILIP)
www.cilip.org.uk
Information on specific standards is available to members of CILIP at:
www.cilip.org.uk/informationadvice/infomanagement/collection/ spaceplanningresources.htm.

Commission for Architecture and the Built Environment (CABE)
Gives advice and guidance for those involved with public buildings.
www.cabe.org.uk

Design Commission for Wales
www.dcfw.org

Design Quality Indicator
'A pioneering process for evaluating design quality of buildings, it can

be used by everyone involved the development process to contribute to improving the quality of our built environment. DQI is a generic toolkit which can be used with all types of building. There is also a version specifically aimed at school buildings.'
www.dqi.org.uk

Designing Libraries Database

For public libraries.

www.designinglibraries.org.uk/

Equal opportunities

Equal opportunities guidance covering access to library services, including buildings.

www.cilip.org.uk/practice/disabled.html.

Libris Design

Libris Design is a US library facility-planning database that assists local library officials with the planning of public library buildings. It provides useful fact sheets on different aspects of library design.

'The Libris Design Project (www.librisdesign.org/) is supported by the U.S. Institute of Museum and Library Services under the provisions of the Library Services and Technology Act, administered in California by the State Librarian.'

http://librisdesign.org/docs/index.html.

The Museums, Libraries and Archives Council (MLA)

Issues guides on making museums, libraries and archives as accessible as possible for disabled people, published by Resource/MLA in 2003/2004.

www.mla.gov.uk/

Office of Government Commerce

Offers guidance to help public sector improve management of projects.

www.ogc.gov.uk

Information on developing a business case at www.ogc.gov.uk/documentation_and_templates_business_case.asp.

Ontario Libraries Clearinghouse of Professional Information

Selection of links to a variety of sources to help libraries in planning and assessing facilities.

www.library.on.ca/links/clearinghouse/facilities/index.htm

Planning and Building Libraries
> This site has been created for librarians, architects, design consultants
> and students interested in all aspects of planning and building
> libraries.
> www.slais.ubc.ca/resources/architecture/index.htm

PRINCE 2 (Project in Controlled Environments)
> Provides a structured methodology for effective project management
> and the UK 'best practice model'.
> www.ogc.gov.uk/methods_prince_2.asp

Public Library Building Awards
> Public Libraries Group of CILIP
> www.cilip.org.uk/specialinterestgroups/bysubject/public/awards

Public Private Partnerships (PPP)
> Information on PPP including the private finance initiative.
> www.hm-treasury.gov.uk/DOCUMENTS/PUBLIC_PRIVATE_
> PARTNERSHIPS/ppp_index.cfm

Royal Institute of British Architects (RIBA)
> www.architecture.com/

SCONUL
> Sconul library building projects database. Includes Library Design
> Awards and building visits web pages. A good source of information
> on recent projects in the academic sector. All these resources can be
> accessed via the Library Buildings section of the SCONUL website.
> www.sconul.ac.uk/lib_build/

Whole Building Design Guide (WBDG)
> A site containing detailed information on the design of a range of public
> buildings. Includes sections on public, school and academic libraries.
> www.wbdg.org

Appendices

Appendix 1

Glossary (including common terms used within the construction/building environment)

This is an alphabetical list of terms that are specific to the construction industry and might be encountered by the librarian as the client in a building project. There may be terms that are not included in the text of this book. This glossary is drawn from several sources, most particularly from CABE's *Creating Excellent Buildings* (Eley, 2003, 183-201).

Access audit A review of the ways in which the building will meet the needs of people with any type of disability. The audit may involve the journey to, entrance into and movement round the building.

Access consultant Specialist in design that enables access for all.

Accessibility Ease of reaching, entering and using a building.

Architect The designer of a building who must be registered with the Architects Registration Board (ARB) in the UK in order to use this designation. The architect often leads the design team, although bigger projects also use project managers who work directly for the client.

Architectural design competitions A means of selection of the design team. The process may add to early costs and extend the timeframe.

Architectural drawing A line drawing - either a plan, section or elevation views of the proposed building.

Area measures   As defined by the Royal Institution of Chartered
Surveyors (RICS):

- gross external area (GEA) – the area enclosed by the outer surface of
the external walls, used for development control and planning
permissions.
- gross internal area (GlA) – the area enclosed by the inner surface of
exterior walls
- net internal area (NIA) – the GIA less internal structure, vertical
circulation (stairs and lifts), plant and WCs
- net useable area (NUA) – the area that can actively be used, equivalent
to the NIA less horizontal circulation routes.

Articles of agreement   The details of a contract.

As-built drawings (also known as Record Drawings)   Contract drawings
marked up to reflect changes made during the construction process.

Axonometric projection   A three-dimensional drawing which combines
the plan and elevations (see also **Isometric projection**).

Benchmark   A standard of performance set by an organization or groups
of common interest, against which similar projects can be measured.

Best value   The value represented by quality and lifetime costs, rather
than construction costs alone. Central and local government clients
are charged with obtaining best value for their construction projects,
as for all other aspects of government, rather than seeking lowest price.
See also **Value for money**.

Bill of quantities   A list of the costs – usually a contract document –
which is calculated by a quantity surveyor (see below) from the
architect's drawings and specifications using a 'standard method of
measurement'. If planned works are changed they are re-measured to
calculate the change in cost.

Brief   Description of what a client wants to include in the project and
how the finished building is to perform (see Chapters 5 and 8).

Budget (construction budget)   An itemized summary of estimated or
intended expenditures for a given period of time. The total sum of
money allocated for a specific project.

Building envelope   The external walls, windows and roof – the waterproof elements of a building. This is sometimes referred to as the building shell.

Building inspector   The person responsible for inspecting building projects on site to ensure that all building regulations are being met. Normally an officer in the local authority.

Building process   A term used to express every step of a construction project from its conception to final acceptance and occupancy.

Building regulations   Statutory requirements to which buildings must conform, aimed primarily at good construction, safety and public protection.

Building surveyor   A surveyor trained in building construction, law and sometimes costing. Often leads the design team for alterations to an existing building.

Business case   The underlying purpose of the project (see Chapter 3).

Capital cost   The total investment needed to complete a project and bring it to a commercially operable status.

Capital grant   A grant towards purchase, construction or refurbishment of buildings (see also **Revenue cost**).

Capital project   One that requires expenditure outside the normal budget for running the organization (the revenue budget).

Certificate – interim and final certificates   Formal documentation issued by the contract administrator to assess progress and authorize payment at set intervals during the construction phase of the project. The final certificate confirms that the contractor appears to have completed the contract satisfactorily and sets out the final contract sum.

Change order   A written document between the owner and the contractor, signed by both, authorizing a change in the work or an adjustment in the contract sum or the contract time. The contract sum and the contract time may be changed only by change order. A change order may be in the form of additional compensation or time.

Claims   Before the final settlement is made, the contractor is likely to review the whole process to see if any additional sums can be 'claimed'. Delays, changes in the specification, unforeseen site problems and so on can all be cited as grounds for a claim if the contractor can show that they were caused by the client or the client's team.

Clerk of works   An on-site representative of the client, architect or contract administrator responsible for verifying and ensuring that what is constructed meets the level of workmanship and materials specified by the design team.

Client   The person or group that 'owns' the building, in this case the library manager.

Client adviser   An independent individual with knowledge of construction and of the business needs and objectives of the client and users.

Client representative   An agent employed by the client to act on his or her behalf but with limited powers. Sometimes also acts as project manager.

Commissioning period   After handover to the client, the period during which the building systems are first used together and small problems are resolved.

Construction costs   Costs of the construction only, excluding items such as land acquisition and legal costs, financing costs, professional fees and VAT. These can include costs for labour, material, equipment, and services; contractors' overheads and other direct construction costs.

Construction design and management (CDM) regulations   These regulations require a client to appoint a planning supervisor to check that construction, site and project health and safety are taken into account throughout the planning and design phases and to co-ordinate the production of the health and safety file.

Construction Industry Council (CIC)   A body whose membership consists of organizations representing the many professional, research and business organizations, as well as individuals, within the construction industry.

Construction management   A form of procurement where the client uses separate contracts to employ a construction manager to manage all processes on site, consultants and specialist contractors or builders.

Contingency   Provision of time or money for unforeseen problems arising during the construction project. The money set aside should form part of a formal risk management strategy.

Contractor   The industry term for a builder. The contractor's role and title depends on the procurement route used:

- main contractor - the organization employed by a client to construct the project
- management contractor - the contractor who employs and manages the construction team, including the specialist contractors
- subcontractors - employed by the main contractors to carry out particular aspects of the construction, e.g. electricians
- specialist subcontractors-contractors in specialized fields likely to do detailed design of the work for which they are responsible, e.g. foundations and air conditioning ductwork.

Cost consultant   A consultant, usually employed by the librarian to estimate or monitor project costs. Usually a professional quantity surveyor, he or she is a specialist in all aspects of the costs of construction, providing information on the likely cost of a project at every stage including cash flow. Can also advise on the form of contract, procurement routes, suitable contractors, inflationary allowances and the need to make contingencies in the cost model.

Critical path   The set of activities that must be completed on time for the project completion date to be met, e.g. raising funds, receiving planning approval and producing information.

DDA see **Disability Discrimination Act 1995**

Defects liability period   A period, usually 12 months, during which the contractor must remedy faults that appear in a building as a result of construction processes (such as cracking of plaster as it dries out).

Design   A graphical representation of plans, elevations and other drawings of the building.

Design and build (D&B)   Method of construction where the constructor or building contractor is partly or entirely responsible for design development and quality as well as for delivery of a building. Variants include design and manage (see below).

Design and manage   A procurement method in which a single body, usually a building contractor, takes sole responsibility for design, management and delivery to the client. The contracts of all consultants and subcontractors are made with this intermediary, rather than with the client.

Design brief   The design brief (sometimes called detailed brief or detailed design brief) is a document describing the 'problem' for which a design provides the 'answer', the demand that the advisers, designers and building contractors must supply. (See also Chapter 8.)

Design, build, finance and operate (DBFO)   This gives private financial partners responsibility to design, build and manage and/or operate the completed facility for many years, usually 20 to 30 years, after which management and operation revert to the client.

Design champion   A person appointed to provide leadership, to generate enthusiasm and commitment to design quality, and to safeguard design quality on behalf of the client. Ideally a senior manager or board member.

Disability Discrimination Act (DDA) 1995   Legislation that progressively requires employers and organizations to meet the needs of disabled staff and users by ensuring full access to their buildings. The final phase came into force in October 2004 when service providers (including libraries) had to have made their premises accessible to disabled customers if it were 'reasonable' to do so.

District surveyor   Although this term is no longer current, it is still sometimes loosely used for the role of building inspector, particularly in London.

Economic impact   The effect of a project on the local economy.

Elevation   A drawing to an accurate scale of any one face of a building or room, viewed as if standing in front of it, with perspective eliminated.

Employer   Another term for the client (librarian).

Enabling works   Building works required before the start of the main construction project, e.g. the demolition of an existing building.

European Union (EU)   EU procedures must be followed for contracts over a certain size that receive more than 50% public funding. The *Official Journal of the European Union* (q.v.) was know as *OJEC* – now it is abbreviated to *OJ* or *OJEU*.

Facilities manager (FM)   The person responsible for managing the operation of the finished building. Although the facilities manager may not be present during the planning stages, that person must still consider the manageability and maintainability of the final building. Sometimes a team has this responsibility.

Fast-track   Techniques to speed up the work and meet tight time requirements, frequently achieved by overlapping design and construction, or prefabricating large components offsite.

Feasibility study   A review carried out early in the process to check whether a set of proposals is likely to fulfil the organization's objectives and whether the chosen site is suitable for the intended building.

Final account   The adjusted contract sum, calculated once the project has been completed, which takes account of all changes to the original tender documents.

Fit-out   The last part of a construction project when the fittings and furniture - carpets, seating, lighting, and so on are installed.

Gantt chart   A visual representation of the schedule of activities for a project. A Gantt chart shows start and finish dates, critical and non-critical activities, slack time and predecessor relationships. It shows the project milestones set against the duration and deadlines for the project.

Gross external area (GEA) see **Area measures**

Gross internal area (GIA) see **Area measures**

Handover   The moment at which responsibility for the completed building, including insurance and management, is passed from the contractor to the client. A full check is needed to ensure that everything promised under the contract has been fulfilled.

Heating, ventilating and air conditioning (HVAC)   Air conditioning controls temperature, cleanliness and humidity of the air. Mechanical 'air handling' or natural ventilation may be used.

Inclusive design   Design that caters fully for all needs and as a minimum meets the requirements of the Disability Discrimination Act (DDA) 1995 (q.v.).

Indirect costs   A contractor's or consultant's overhead expenses; expenses indirectly incurred and not chargeable to a specific project or task. They are also known as soft costs.

Integrated process   Collaborative techniques to unite the client, designers and builders with the aim of increasing efficiency and harmonizing processes, e.g. ICT systems or software.

Integrated team; integrated supply team (IST)   The designer, contractor and client who work together from the start to achieve the agreed objectives of the project.

Interior designer   A specialist trained in design for fit-out, but not for building construction.

Invitation to tender see **Tender process**

Isometric projection   A three-dimensional geometrical drawing in which the plan is distorted but verticals remain vertical and to scale. Gives a more realistic 'view' than an axonometric projection (q.v.) but with more distortion of relative sizes.

Key performance indicators (KPIs)   Benchmarks based on information from many projects assessing success. Those available from the Construction Industry Council cover many process issues, including client and user satisfaction.

Landscape architect   Specialist in landscape design, construction or horticulture.

Latent defects   These are building defects that appear after completion. They are covered by Limitation Acts, which state a time limit after which claims cannot be brought for errors in design and construction. If, during this period, the client can prove that the design or construction team is responsible for any defect, they will normally be liable for losses suffered by the client as a result.

Legibility   The ease with which one can find one's way around a building.

Life cycle or life time costs see **Whole life costs**

Liquidated and ascertained damages (Lads)   A realistic estimate of the losses that the client believes will ensue as a result of delay in completing the project. This estimate is included in the contract as a sum of money per week for which the contractor will be liable if the project runs over time. Damages cannot be claimed from contractors for delays beyond their control.

Long-life loose fit   This indicates that a building may meet evolving needs more easily if the design is not over-specific.

Lump-sum contract   A contract for a fixed sum including all costs associated with the construction. Should only be calculated on a finalized and fully detailed design.

Manageability   The ease of managing a building over its lifetime in terms of its everyday operation.

Management by exception   A technique whereby senior managers set thresholds to which the project manager or team can work. Anything that exceeds a threshold will be referred to the senior manager.

Management contracting   A procurement method where a contractor is chosen at an early stage and acts in a management capacity before construction starts. Often this contractor only manages the building works carried out by other subcontractors. Also known as 'fast-track' procurement because the contractor can start site works as soon as there is sufficient information, leaving the design team to prepare the rest of the design information.

Mechanical and electrical (M&E) services   Mechanical and electrical services include power and data supply, lighting, air conditioning, humidity control, plumbing and drainage. M&E are designed and specified by services engineers.

Net internal area (NIA) see **Area measures**

Net present value (NPV)   The current value of a project across its lifetime, at agreed discount rates.

Net usable area (NUA) see **Area measures**

Nominated subcontractor   A specialist subcontractor chosen by the client and nominated using special provisions in the contract, who must be used by the contractor.

Office of Government Commerce (OGC)   Part of HM Treasury, OGC works to improve procurement and project management. It also works with suppliers to make the government marketplace more efficient and attractive to business.

The Official Journal of the European Union (OJ)   Formerly known as *OJEC*. Daily journal advertising the service requirements of all public procurement, including construction projects. Publicly funded projects over a certain size must advertise here for professional teams and builders.

Option appraisal/analysis   Before agreeing the building project several alternatives should be appraised to ensure the right strategy is adopted, typically between three and five options, including a 'do nothing' option. Analysis of the options may give different weightings to various qualities. It may be decided during this process that a building project is not the best way to achieve the agreed objectives.

Organizational capacity   A shorthand way of describing the ability of an organization to plan and carry out a capital project. The main qualities needed for building projects are strategic management, financial control and executive leadership.

Orientation   The planning of a building in relation to its surroundings, usually described in terms of its compass setting, e.g. south-facing garden, north–south orientation.

Outline brief   An initial description of the client goals and requirements, which forms the basis for feasibility studies and decisions about the project. Sometimes described as a strategic brief or a statement of needs or requirements.

Outline planning permission/consent   Outline permission can be sought for a building before detailed designs have been proposed, based on an outline scheme. Normally full planning permission is sought after discussion to determine the likely acceptability of the project. (See also **Planning permission**.)

Output specification   The form in which briefs may be stated. Essential for PFI projects, it requests the provision of the service that the building will provide, rather than describing the accommodation.

Out-turn costs   The total or projected cost of a project including land acquisition, construction and fitting-out costs, professional fees, contingencies, disruption and financing costs, VAT and inflation. The total sum the budget must cover.

Partnering   Co-operation between the various contractors, consultants and employers for mutual benefit. It is not a procurement route but a flexible definition of approach. Framework agreements are often the outcome of a partnering approach.

Performance specifications   The written material containing the minimum acceptable standards and actions, as may be necessary to complete a project. Including the minimum acceptable quality standards and aesthetic values expected upon completion of the project.

Plan   The layout of a building taking a horizontal slice and showing everything through which the cut passes.

Planning permission   Permission that must be obtained from the local authority before construction starts on most projects. It controls the proposed use, how much of the site is covered, the size of the building, site access, external landscape and parking, and conformity with existing local plans. If permission is not granted, an appeal may be heard by a public enquiry and determined by a planning inspector. The Secretary of State for the Environment makes the final decision.

Post-project evaluation and post occupancy evaluation (POE)   End of project assessment of both the process and the completed building. A post-project evaluation of the process can be carried out soon after hand-over, but post-occupancy evaluation should be carried out later, when it is possible to assess how well the building fulfils the client's aims and objectives (see Chapter 11). The purpose of the evaluation is to identify necessary remedial actions and to document how the process could be improved in the future.

Practical completion   A certificate is generally issued by the architect, certifying satisfactory completion of the construction – that the building is capable of delivering the activity for which it was designed. It normally allows the contractor to invoice the client for all but a small portion of the contract sum. The outstanding portion is called the retention (q.v.) and is usually released after a 12-month period once the main contractor has corrected all building construction defects that have emerged.

Preliminaries (Prelims)   Preliminary clauses in a cost document or tender that set out general conditions that may have cost implications, e.g. standards, sites access, hours of working. The word also refers to the cost of the contractor maintaining a site presence, e.g. the cost of renting temporary buildings, insurance.

Pre-qualification   This is sometimes called qualification. The process by which a contractor or design team is deemed competent to be placed on a short list for possible selection for a project. The conditions for suitability should include assessment of competence as indicated by track record, size, staff qualifications and financial record.

Primary contract   A design and build contractor with a supply chain of reliable suppliers of quality products.

Prior indicative notice (PIN)   The notification that must be sent to the *Official Journal of the European Union* (q.v.) announcing that suppliers will be sought for publicly funded projects or services above specific values.

Private finance initiative (PFI)   A procurement route in which a private sector supplier takes over the design, construction and management of a building for use by the public sector. The typical operating period is 20 to 30 years. Outputs must be clearly defined. At the end of the operating period, ownership of the building reverts to the public sector.

Procurement route   The method by which the consultancy, building contract and related services are tendered and purchased. Procurement routes range from traditional to PFI, with many variations in between.

Professional indemnity (PI) insurance   The insurance that some professionals must have to protect them against alleged negligent behaviour that causes losses to the client, often due to defects to the building, delays to the programme or injury.

Project brief see **Brief**

Project delivery team   Designers, contractors and all other specialists working to design and deliver the building to meet the client's brief.

Project directory   A written list of all parties connected with a specific project. The list usually includes a classification or description of the party, e.g. architect, civil engineer, and full contact details.

Project integration management   The process whereby alternative objectives or methods are considered and their benefits and problems are traded off against each other with a view to getting the optimum result, often as a result of an option appraisal (see above).

Project manager   A specialist given day-to-day management of the building team, co-ordinating timetables and maintaining appropriate communication channels. The client's project manager safeguards the client's interest at all times, ensuring that the project is completed within budget, on time and to the right level of quality. The project delivery team will have its own project manager.

Project sponsor   The individual charged with representing the client and carrying out client responsibilities. The project sponsor communicates with the client body and encourages dialogue between the client and other players to ensure that the client's needs are understood and met.

Project team, project delivery team   The entire team, including both design and construction, and any specialists who are working to design and deliver the project for the client.

Public–Private Partnerships (PPP)   Procurement methods that involve working in partnership with private finance. They usually involve versions of design and build (q.v.) including prime contracting. Public–private partnerships (PPPs) are arrangements typified by joint working between the public and private sector. In the broadest sense, PPPs can cover all types of collaboration across the interface between the public and private sectors to deliver policies, services and infrastructure. Where delivery of public services involves private sector investment in infrastructure, the most common form of PPP is the Private Finance Initiative [q.v.].

Public sector comparator   A cost estimate based on the assumption that a project will be constructed in a conventional way, to use as a benchmark against which to assess the net present value of PFI bids, in order check that procurement through PFI is providing value for money.

Quality-based selection (QBS)   Selection of service and products on the basis of appropriate quality, not of lowest cost.

Quantity surveyor see **Cost consultant**

Radio frequency identification (RFID)   A wireless data collection technology that uses electronic tags for storing data. Like barcodes, they are used to identify items. Unlike barcodes, which must be brought close to the scanner for reading, RFID tags are read when they are within the proximity of a transmitted radio signal.

Request for information (RFI)   A written request from a contractor to the owner or architect for clarification or information about the contract documents following contract award.

Retention   A percentage of the construction cost, usually between 2% and 5%, which is retained during construction and for a period following handover. This obliges the contractor to rectify small construction defects that appear as the building is used.

Revenue cost   Revenue cost covers the costs of using and running a building, including rent, rates, insurance, utilities, maintenance and staff costs.

Risk assessment or risk management   Identification of potential project risks and a strategy to address them.

Room data sheet   A list of requirements for a given room, including furniture, equipment, power and telecommunications cables, finishes and fittings.

Schedule of rates   Contractors commonly provide tender prices as a 'schedule of rates' where particular building tasks are costed at a standard rate per metre or square metre, e.g. laying floor tiles. The schedule is usually included as part of the contract and may also be used with the bill of quantities (q.v.).

Scheme design study (or detailed proposal)   Additional technical information that may be required for funding applications for larger projects, including plans, specifications, sections and elevations, and a cost estimate.

Section   The vertical layout of a building taking a vertical slice and showing everything through which the cut passes.

Section 106 agreements   Agreements whereby planning permission is granted subject to the developer or client fulfilling certain conditions, e.g. local road improvements.

Senior responsible owner (SRO)   A central government term for the senior manager in the business unit that requires the project who has status and authority to provide leadership.

Sensitivity analysis   A test of the effect that different assumptions have on the 'bottom line'. Often used as part of the business case of the project (q.v.).

Services engineer   Sometimes called an environmental engineer. Specialists in the design of mechanical and electrical systems, air handling, energy conservation, lighting, drainage, acoustics, fire, etc. Although many engineers focus on a single field, large engineering firms cover the range of services required by complex projects. For smaller, less complex projects, the architect's team may provide the services engineer.

Shell and core   Description of a building completed only to the stage where the outer shell and the core (boilers and other building equipment, and vertical circulation stairs and lifts), plus in some cases ceiling and floor finishes, basic lighting and services are provided. This allows the client to subdivide the space and finish it to specific requirements (e.g. for a tenant).

Signing off   A process of formally recording the client's approval of briefing statements or design proposals.

Snagging   The process of identifying and fixing defects prior to project completion. The responsibility for remedying these normally lies primarily with the contractor. The project timetable should always allow time for snagging before moving in. However, some items, such as air handling systems, can only be fully tested after running through all seasons of the year.

Specialist subcontractor   An organization employed to handle a specialized aspect of the building, such as ductwork or foundations, and which usually has a role in designing, supplying and fixing the elements in which it specializes.

Specification   The technical description used to set the standards of materials, workmanship and type of construction.

Stakeholder   People and groups who are affected by, or have a financial or practical interest in, the outcome of a project.

Statement of need (SON) or statement of requirements (SOR)   Another term for an outline brief. Often this is a formal statement that must be signed off by a board or senior member of the organization before the project process can start.

Strategic brief see **Outline brief**

Structural engineer   Specialist in the design of building structures.

Decisions about the type of structure are integral to the design and should be taken with the architect. The engineer is responsible for ensuring that the structure has the appropriate strength and integrity.

Supply chain   This is made up of all the parties responsible for delivering a specific product or service. There may be a number of specialized supply chains and the members of each should be accustomed to working together as a fully linked chain.

Surveyor   A surveyor measures and maps out various aspects of land and buildings, for example in relation to dimensions, costs and construction.

Sustainable materials   Resources that will not be exhausted. For example, timber from renewable forests is sustainable, while that from slow-growing tropical hardwoods is not. Good design should incorporate sustainability, reducing waste and promoting a healthy environment.

Tender process   This is the process of inviting organizations to submit a proposal, with costs, to carry out a piece of work. It covers the preliminary invitation to tender, formal invitation to tender and the actual form of tender.

User champion   Person representing a group of users, transmitting their needs to the design team and informing the group about project progress, including for fit out and move in.

Users   All the people who will use the building, including library staff, tenants and users.

Value for money   The central government term expressing the goal to be achieved by balancing quality time and cost in a construction project. See also **Best value**.

Value management or value engineering   A formalized approach to managing a project through its whole life that seeks best value for money. Multi-disciplinary workshops can be organized to determine whether better value solutions are possible within the constraints of the brief and the project.

Variation   A statement of the costs associated with changes to the contracted works.

Vision statement   Main objectives, needed for early consensus to be able to start the feasibility and budget checks and as a constant reference point throughout the project. The vision develops alongside a 'statement of need', and design quality needs to be part of it.

Whole life costs   The full cost of all the parts that go to make up a building, including initial capital costs, replacement costs, maintenance and repair costs. Sometimes referred to as life cycle costs.

Whole life value   Value of an asset when its whole life costs are taken into account. Sustainability is an important aspect of whole life value.

Working drawings   The detailed drawings showing how the different parts of the building are joined together and used by construction teams on site or when preparing off site assembly of parts.

Appendix 2

Ambience – discussion checklist for librarians and architects

Modernization of libraries
- image of library service and marketing/consultation
- design – responding to lifestyle change
- resources and services
- staff skills and customer care
- buildings/facilities/presentation and layout
- retail approach to be adopted, for example:
  - bookshops that display and sell books
  - other retail responses to market forces and leisure retailers (like Nike, Apple stores) with a wider product range than bookshops - rather like libraries
  - other sectors that libraries can refer to, in addition to retail, for example sports, health

Inside the library
- how the layout and presentation could hinder or help
- how design improvements could be made, e.g.:
  - need to circulate clockwise
  - use of open spaces

Entrance areas

- systems and procedures before products and services
- passages and corridors
- posters or plasma screen
- presumption of confidence and familiarity
- vestiges of 'no entry without a ticket' attitude
- restriction of spontaneity
- entrance area as event or performance space

Reception/greeting points

- impressions
- size and function of counters – for customers or storage?
- windbreaks and screens
- alternatives

Sight lines

- being able to see where users are going
- establishing clear sight lines
- gathering points
- staff availability for help

Creating space

- a fresh assessment of time-honoured use
- examining what is flexible in the building's structure

Use of space

- arriving
- learning
- studying
- privacy
- browsing – new groupings/arrangements of stock
- reading and relaxing/resting
- information
- younger children
- older children/young adults

- different ambiences for different spaces
- positioning of different spaces
- events and activities
- public art

Guiding

- clear/flexible
- visible
- attractive and dyslexia friendly – mix of very visible text and images
- house style

Furniture

- interior design ideas in support of use of space
- presentation of posters/leaflets
- displays
- replacement
- group seating
- study
- sofa/easy chairs

Shelving

- mobility and flexibility
- open/closed access
- age groups
- disability

Equipment

- PCs
- photocopier
- baskets and personal trolleys

Facilities

- refreshments/café
- vending area
- use of mobile phones

Colour and images

- reflecting diversity
- community of interest
- overall style to complement space/purpose

Lighting schemes

- variable/flexible

Events and activities

- transforming space for events and performances

Appendix 3

Top ten tips

Top ten tips

. . . for ensuring that communities and individuals engage with new library spaces.

(As agreed by library managers/local staff from Birmingham, Solihull, Telford & Wrekin, Warwickshire and Worcestershire and colleagues from MLA, the Big Lottery and Warwick University Business School – at a workshop organized by MLA West Midlands on 13 June 2007)

1 Have the right staff – well motivated, knowledgeable and from diverse backgrounds.
2 Act on what communities are saying – and tell them what you are doing.
3 Design buildings for 'community' roles – develop multi-functional spaces.
4 Market effectively from the outset – and continue a dialogue with users and non-users.
5 Create attractive spaces – clean, lighted, signed (with contemporary decor and coffee!).
6 Involve staff in planning for success – and from the very start of the renewal of a space.

7 Future-proof – be flexible, be aware of trends and plan to be ICT/media rich.
8 Make the most of partnerships within and beyond the local authority – avoid the silo mentality.
9 Welcome the architect into the team – not as the enemy but as an equal partner.
10 Look beyond the books/resources – recognize the individual and cater for personalization.

Appendix 4

Space adjacencies diagram

Seattle Public Library Neighborhood Branches
Universal Building Program
Space Adjacencies Diagram

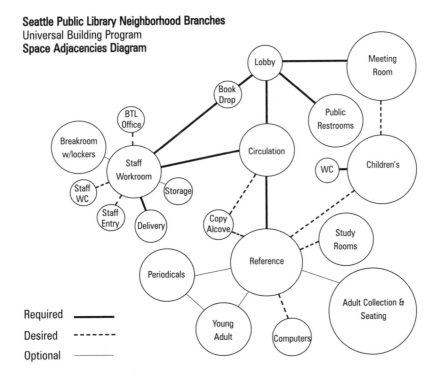

Required ——————
Desired ------
Optional ——————

Source:

www.spl.lib.wa.us/lfa/universalbranchbldgprogram/adjacenciesdiagram.jpg

Index

success
  business case 21–3
  project management 39
summary, building libraries
    143–5

team, design/project see
    design/project team
technical considerations, interior
    design 109
technical terms xvii–xix
ten commandments, building
    design 104–5
tendering
  services 69–71
  works 69–71
texts, further reading 147–55
time management, project
    management 32–4

top ten tips 183–4
traditional v modern architecture
    7–8

urban design, design quality 97–8
use data, space planning 123–5
use of space, discussion checklist
    180–1
user seating space 127
users, library, team role 50

virtual libraries 12–13

websites
  further reading 155–7
  project management 34–5
work stages, design/project team
    53–6
works, tendering 69–71

Libraries Designed for Kids
Nolan Lushington

How do you set about planning and designing a library for children or teenagers? How should it be different from a library intended for adults, and how can you get the right kind of help from designers and architects?

Get the 'inside story' from an experienced library design consultant on creating those special spaces in your library that promote and encourage children's and young adults' curiosity, learning, and reading – and support their lifelong love of books and information.

Nolan Lushington covers the complete planning process from concept to 'grand opening', guiding you through the technical aspects of design and construction and the finer points of lighting, acoustics, furnishings, equipment, multimedia areas, youth areas, and much more. Key topics include:

- improving service by design
- innovative children's library models
- planning a new children's library
- assessing physical needs
- design considerations
- organizing the children's area
- entrances, displays, graphics and lighting
- age-related design
- designing programme, activity and staff areas
- furnishings and equipment
- quick fixes and common mistakes.

The helpful appendices offer case studies and lists of suppliers, architects and further information.

Whether you're a children's or youth librarian, library director, school facilities planner – or indeed an architect or designer – you'll discover valuable, practical tips and insights to help you create that inviting environment called the library.

Nolan Lushington is a library design consultant and President of Lushington Consultants, Hartford CT. He is Chairman of the American Library Association Buildings and Equipment Section and a juror of the ALA Building Awards.

2008; 184pp; paperback; 978-1-85604-657-2; £44.95

CILIP: taking you where you want to be

Is job satisfaction important to you? Would you like greater recognition within your organisation? Are you hoping to progress up the career ladder?

If your answer is yes to one or more of these questions CILIP can help.

We believe that job satisfaction comes from doing a job to the best of your ability and from getting recognition from your manager, your colleagues and your customers.

By investing in CILIP membership you can benefit from a range of services, including new online content, which will help you do your job better and enhance your career prospects.

For your free membership pack, email findoutmore@cilip.org.uk today.

Chartered Institute of
Library and Information
Professionals

www.cilip.org.uk/member
Now even more reasons to belong